SECOND CATECHISM,

SCRIPTURAL PROOFS.

---

1. *WHAT* is *God?*

God is *an infinite* and *eternal Spirit*, is everywhere present, can do whatever he will, knows every *thought* in man's heart, every word, and every action, is *holy* and *righteous*, *faithful* and *true*, *gracious* and *merciful*, the one only *living* and *true* God, in three *persons*, the same in *substance*, *equal* in power and glory, who should be thought of with *fear* and *love*, who should be spoken of with *reverence* and *praise*.

1. *God is infinite.* Job xi. 7. Canst thou by searching find out God? Canst thou find out the Almighty unto perfection?

2. *God is eternal.* Psalm xc. 2. From everlasting to everlasting thou art God.

3. *God is a Spirit.* John iv. 24. God is a Spirit.

4. *God is everywhere present.* Jer. xxiii. 24. Do not I fill heaven and earth? saith the Lord.

5. *God can do whatever he will.* Job xlii. 2. I know that thou canst do every thing.

6. *God knows all things.* Psalm cxxxix. 2, 3. Thou knowest my downsitting and mine uprising; thou understandest my thought afar off. Thou compassest my path and my lying down, and art acquainted with all my ways.

7. *God is holy.* Rev. xv. 4. Thou only art holy.

8. *God is righteous.* Psalm cxlv. 17. The Lord is righteous in all his ways.

9. *God is faithful.* Num. xxiii. 19. God is not a man that he should lie.

10. *God is true.* Deut. xxxii. 4. A God of truth, and without iniquity; just and right is he.

11. *God is gracious.* Psalm cxlv. 9. The Lord is good to all; and his tender mercies are over all his works.

---

1. *An infinite,* One whose attributes are not limited by any imperfection or defect. *Eternal,* Who is without beginning and without end. *Spirit,* A thinking being without bodily substance. *Thought,* Imagination or desire. *Holy,* Free from all sin or impurity. *Righteous,* Just and equitable. *Faithful,* Firmly adhering to his determination. *True,* Opposing and hating all that is false or feigned. *Gracious,* Condescendingly kind. *Merciful,* Compassionate and forgiving. *Living,* Self-existent. *Persons,* Distinct individuals. *Substance,* Being or existence. *Equal,* Exactly alike. *Fear,* Holy awe. *Love,* Filial affection. *Reverence,* Feelings of the most profound veneration. *Praise,* Unqualified approbation.

12. *God is merciful.* Exod. xxxiv. 6. The Lord, The Lord God merciful and gracious.

13. *God is one.* Deut. vi. 4. Hear, O Israel, The Lord our God i one Lord.

14. *God is the only living and true God.* Jer. x. 10. The Lord the true God, he is the living God, and an everlasting King.

15. *There are three persons in the Godhead.* 1 John v. 7. For ther are three that bear record in heaven, the Father, the Word, and th Holy Ghost.

16. *These three are the same in substance.* 1 John v. 7. Thes three are one.

17. *These three are equal in power.* John v. 21. As the Fathe raiseth up the dead and quickeneth them, even so the Son quickenet whom he will.

18. *These three are equal in glory.* Matt. xxviii. 19. Go ye there fore and teach all nations, baptizing them in the name of the Father and of the Son, and of the Holy Ghost.

19. *God should be thought of with fear.* Jer. x. 7. Who would no fear thee, O King of nations, for to thee doth it appertain.

20. *God should be thought of with love.* Matt. xxii. 37. Thou sha love the Lord thy God with all thy heart, and with all thy soul, an with all thy mind.

21. *God should be spoken of with reverence.* Psalm lxxxix. 7. Go is greatly to be feared in the assembly of the saints, and to be had reverence of all them that are about him.

22. *God should be spoken of with praise.* Psalm lxvii. 3. Let th people praise thee, O God. Let all the people praise thee.

2. *What is Man?*

Man is a *creature of* God, for he *made* him, both body an soul: the soul is *that within him*, which *thinks* and *know wishes* and *desires*, *rejoices* and is *sorry*, which is a *spiri* and will *live* after the body is dead, and which is more va luable than the *whole world* ; the body, which is the *outwar frame*, is made of flesh and blood, and will *die.*

1. *Man is a creature of God.* Isa. xlv. 11, 12. Thus saith th Lord,—I have made the earth, and created man upon it.

2. *God created man's body.* Job x. 11. Thou hast clothed me wit skin and flesh, and hast fenced me with bones and sinews.

3. *God created man's soul.* Zech. xii. 1. The Lord,—formeth th spirit of man within him.

4. *The soul within man thinks and knows, wishes and desires, re joices and is sorry.* Job xxxii. 8. There is a spirit in man; and th inspiration of the Almighty giveth them understanding.

5. *The soul of man is a spirit.* Luke xxiv. 39. A spirit hath no flesh and bones.

6. *The soul shall live after the body is dead.* Eccles. xii. 7. The

---

2. *Creature of,* Being who owes his existence to. *Made,* Contrived and formed *That within him,* That spiritual intelligence. *Thinks,* Reflects. *Knows,* Per ceives. *Wishes,* Longs for. *Desires,* Earnestly solicits to be gratified. *Rejoice* Feels and expresses pleasurable sensations. *Sorry,* Grieved by unpleasant occur rences. *Live,* Survive. *Whole world,* Globe we inhabit, with all its riches. *Out ward frame,* Tenement of the soul. *Die,* Be deprived by death of its present e istence.

shall the dust return to the earth as it was; and the spirit shall return unto God who gave it.

7. *The soul is of more value than the whole world.* Mark viii. 36. What shall it profit a man if he shall gain the whole world and lose his own soul.

8. *The body is the outward frame.* Job. x. 11. Thou hast clothed me with skin and flesh, and hast fenced me with bones and sinews.

9. *The body is made of flesh and blood.* 2. Sam. xix. 12. Ye are my brethren, ye are my bones and my flesh.

10. *The body will die.* Matt. x. 28. Fear not them which kill the body, but are not able to kill the soul.

3. *Did God create any thing besides man ?*

God *created* the *heavens* and the *earth*, and *all things* that are *therein*, for the *manifestation* of his *glory*, and to give *happiness* to *his creatures ;* he *preserves* all things which he has *made*, and all the *good things we enjoy come from him.*

1. *God created the heavens and the earth.* Gen. i. 1. In the beginning God created the heaven and the earth.

2. *God created all things in heaven and in earth.* John i. 3. All things were made by him ; and without him was not any thing made that was made.

3. *God created all things for the manifestation of his glory.* Psalm xix. 1. The heavens declare the glory of God, and the firmament showeth his handywork.

4. *God made all things so as to impart happiness to his creatures.* Psalm xxxiii. 5. The earth is full of the goodness of the Lord.

5. *God preserves all things which he has made.* Psalm cxlv. 15. The eyes of all wait upon thee ; and thou givest them their meat in due season.

6. *God is the giver of all the good things we enjoy.* Acts xvii. 28. In him we live and move and have our being.

4. *Has man served the end for which he was created ?*

Our *first parents* fell from that holy and happy *state* in which they were *created*, by the sin of eating the *forbidden fruit*, which God, to try them whether they would *obey him* or not, commanded them not to eat, and by their *unbelief* and *disobedience* they *incurred* the *displeasure* of God, to whom, as their *creator, benefactor*, and *governor*, they ought to have

3. *Created*, Brought into existence. *Heavens*, Celestial bodies with which we are surrounded. *Earth*, Globe consisting of land and water, on which we dwell. *All things*, Every creature, whether animate or inanimate. *Therein*, Found in them or upon them. *Manifestation*, Display. *Glory*, Wisdom, power, and goodness. *Happiness*, Felicity. *His creatures*, The beings which he had brought into existence. *Preserves*, Keeps in being, and prevents from falling back into nothing. *Made*, Contrived and formed. *Good things*, Blessings, whether of providence or grace. *We enjoy*, From which we derive pleasure or advantage. *Come from him*, Proposed from God.

4. *Our first parents*, Adam and Eve, the common parents of mankind. *State*, Condition. *Created*, First made. *Forbidden fruit*, Fruit of a tree in the garden of Eden. *Obey him*, Prefer his will when opposed to their own inclinations. *Unbelief*, Want of faith in his threatenings. *Disobedience*, Opposition to his will. *Incurred*, Brought down. *Displeasure*, Disapprobation and curse. *Creator*, Maker. *Benefactor*, Providential preserver. *Governor*, Rightful sovereign. *Implicitly*

implicitly submitted themselves; and *thus,* by their fall, ma
kind was brought into a state of *sin* and *misery.*

1. *Our first parents were created holy and happy.* Gen. i. 27. C
created man in his own image.

2. *Our first parents fell from the state in which they were created*
eating the forbidden fruit. Gen. iii. 6. When the woman saw t
the tree was good for food, and that it was pleasant to the eyes,
a tree to be desired to make one wise, she took of the fruit ther
and did eat, and gave also unto her husband with her, and he did

3. *God commanded our first parents not to eat the forbidden fru*
to try them whether they would obey him or not. Gen. ii. 17. Of
tree of the knowledge of good and evil thou shalt not eat of it.

4. *Our first parents, by their unbelief and disobedience, incurred*
displeasure of God. Gen. iii. 17. And unto Adam he said, Beca
thou hast hearkened unto the voice of thy wife, and hast eaten of
tree of which I commanded thee, saying, Thou shalt not eat of
cursed is the ground for thy sake.

5. *Our first parents ought to have submitted themselves to G*
Gen. ii. 17. In the day that thou eatest thereof thou shalt surely

6. *God as their creator was entitled to their submission.* Isa. xlii
I have created him for my glory.

7. *God as their benefactor was entitled to their submission.* Isa.
Hear, O heavens, and give ear, O earth; for the Lord hath spok
I have nourished and brought up children, and they have rebe
against me.

8. *God as their governor was entitled to their submission.* L
xix. 27. But those mine enemies which would not that I should re
over them, bring hither and slay them before me.

9. *Our first parents by their fall brought mankind into a state*
sin. Rom. v. 12. By one man sin entered into the world, and de
by sin.

10. *Our first parents by their fall brought mankind into a state*
misery. Rom. v. 17. By one man's offence, death reigned by one

5. *Wherein consists the sinfulness of that state into wh*
man fell?

The sinfulness of that state into which man fell, cons
in the want of *original righteousness,* and the *corruption*
his whole nature, which is commonly called original sin,
gether with all the *actual* transgressions which *proceed fr*
it.

1. *The sinfulness of our fallen state consists in the want of orig*
righteousness. Rom. iii. 10. There is none righteous, no not one

2. *The sinfulness of our fallen state consists in the corruptio*
our whole nature. Psalm li. 5. Behold I was shapen in iniquity,
in sin did my mother conceive me.

Without hesitation or inquiry. *Submitted themselves,* Yielded a cheerful obedie
Thus, In this manner. *Mankind,* All the human race. *Sin,* Alienation from
Misery, A state of unhappiness and suffering.

5. *Original righteousness,* Those good dispositions which Adam had when Go
first made him. *Corruption,* Depravity and wickedness. *His whole nature,*
his faculties and powers, both of body and soul. *Actual,* Real and pers
Proceed from it, Flow or come from original sin,

3. The sinfulness in our fallen state is shewn in our actual transgressions. Eccles. vii. 20. There is not a just man upon earth that doeth good and sinneth not.

4. Actual transgressions proceed from original sin. The wicked are estranged from the womb, they go astray as soon as they be born, speaking lies. Psalm lviii. 3.

6. *In what consists the misery of that state into which man fell?*

All mankind being born in sin, and *following the devices and desires* of their own corrupt hearts, are under the *wrath and curse* of God, and so are made *liable* to the *miseries of this life*, to death itself, and to the pains of hell *hereafter*.

1. *Man is born in sin.* Psalm li. 5. Behold I was shapen in iniquity, and in sin did my mother conceive me.

2. *Man follows the devices and desires of his own corrupt heart.* Rom. i.

3. *Man is under the wrath and curse of God.* The carnal mind is enmity against God, for it is not subject to the law of God, neither indeed can be. Eph. ii. 3. And were by nature the children of wrath even as others.

4. *Man is liable to the miseries of this life.* Job. v. 7. Man is born unto trouble as the sparks fly upward.

5. *Man is liable to death.* Rom. vi. 23. The wages of sin is death.

6. *Man is liable to the pains of hell.* Psalm ix. 17. The wicked shall be turned into hell; and all the nations that forget God.

7. *How were our first parents led to commit sin?*

Our first parents were *led* to commit sin against God by the *subtlety* of the devil, who made use of the serpent to *beguile* Eve.

1. *Our first parents committed sin against God.* Rom. v. 18. By the offence of one, judgment came upon all men to condemnation.

2. *Our first parents were led to commit sin by the subtlety of the devil.* Gen. iii. 13. And the woman said, The serpent beguiled me and I did eat.

3. *The devil made use of the serpent to beguile Eve.* Gen. iii. 4, 5. And the serpent said unto the woman, Ye shall not surely die, for God doth know, that in the day ye eat thereof, then your eyes shall be opened, and ye shall be as gods, knowing good and evil.

8. *Who is the devil?*

The devil is the *chief* of the fallen angels, who, before the creation of man, sinned against God, and were *cast* out of

---

6. *Born in sin*, Sinful and guilty when they come into the world. *Following*, Yielding a willing obedience to. *Devices*, Inventions, contrivances. *Desires*, Inclinations. *Corrupt*, Depraved and wicked to. *Wrath*, Anger. *Curse*, Sentence to misery. *Liable*, Subject to. *Miseries*, Things which make men unhappy. *Hereafter*, Throughout all eternity. *This present*, This life. *State of existence.*

7. *Led*, Induced. *Commit*, To be guilty of. *Subtlety*, Artful malevolence. *Beguile*, Impose upon. *Guilty*, Sinned against. *Against God*, Acted in opposition to the will of.

8. *Chief*, Principal. *Cast*,

heaven, and who are *reserved* to the *judgment* of the *great day*, whose *employment* is to *tempt* men to *sin*, by putting evil *thoughts* and *desires* into their *minds*, and to lead them to *their own place of misery: wicked people* are *under the power* of the devil, yet he *cannot do* what he *pleases*, for God *controls his power*, and will *save* from his *malice* and *subtlety* all those who *put their trust* in him.

1. *The devil is the chief of the fallen angels.* Matt. xxv. 41. Depart from me, ye cursed, into everlasting fire, prepared for the devil and his angels.

2. *The fallen angels, before the creation of man, sinned against God.* John viii. 44. Ye are of your father the devil, and the lusts of your father ye will do: he was a murderer from the beginning, and abode not in the truth.

3. *The fallen angels were cast out of heaven.* Jude 6. The angels which kept not their first estate.

4. *The fallen angels are reserved to the judgment of the great day.* Jude 6. The angels which kept not their first estate, but left their own habitation, he hath reserved in everlasting chains, under darkness unto the judgment of the great day.

5. *The employment of the fallen angels is to tempt men to sin.* 1 Pet. v. 8. Be sober, be vigilant, because your adversary the devil, as a roaring lion, walketh about seeking whom he may devour.

6. *The fallen angels tempt men to sin by putting into their minds evil thoughts and desires.* Eph. ii. 2. Wherein in time past ye walked according to the course of this world, according to the prince of the power of the air, the spirit that now worketh in the children of disobedience.

7. *The fallen angels are employed in leading men to their own place of misery.* Rev. xx. 9, 10. And fire came down from God out of heaven and devoured them: and the devil that deceived them was cast into the lake of fire and brimstone.

8. *Wicked people are under the power of the devil.* 2 Tim. ii. 26. And that they may recover themselves out of the snare of the devil who are taken captive by him at his will.

9. *The devil cannot do what he pleases.* Luke xxii. 31, 32. Satan hath desired to have you, that he may sift you as wheat; but I have prayed for thee that thy faith fail not.

10. *God controls the power of the devil.* 1 Cor. x. 13. But God is faithful, who will not suffer you to be tempted above that ye are able.

11. *God will save from the malice and subtlety of the devil, those who put their trust in him.* Prov. xxix. 25. Whoso putteth his trust in the Lord shall be safe.

Driven. *Reserved*, Kept from their final destiny. *Judgment*, Decision. *Great day*, Day when the eternal state of every intelligent being will be irrevocably fixed. *Employment*, Daily and hourly occupation. *Tempt*, Induce. *Sin*, Neglect or disobey the commandments of God. *Thoughts*, Imaginations. *Desires*, Inclinations. *Minds*, Understandings and Affections. *Their own place of misery*, Hell. *Wicked people*, Ungodly sinners. *Under the power*, Subject to the authority. *Cannot do*, Is unable to perform. *Pleases*, Wills and desires. *Controls his power*, Holds his authority in subjection. *Save*, Protect and deliver. *Malice*, Evil intentions. *Subtlety*, Artful malevolence. *Put their trust*, Implicitly confide.

9. *Who is the Redeemer of man?*

The Redeemer of man is our Lord Jesus Christ, the *eternal Son of God*, and the second person in the *glorious Trinity*, who became man, and so was, and continueth to be God and man, in two *distinct* natures, and one *person*, for ever.

1. *Jesus Christ is the Redeemer of men.* Gal. iv. 4, 5. God sent forth his Son made of a woman, made under the law, to redeem them that were under the law.

2. *Jesus Christ is the eternal Son of God.* Heb. i. 8. Unto the Son he saith, Thy throne, O God, is for ever and ever.

3. *Jesus Christ is the second person in the Trinity.* Matt. xxviii. 19. Go ye therefore and teach all nations, baptizing them in the name of the Father, and of the Son, and of the Holy Ghost.

4. *Jesus Christ became man.* Heb. ii. 16. He took not on him the nature of angels, but he took on him the seed of Abraham.

5. *Jesus Christ possesses the nature of God and man in one person.* 1 Tim. iii. 16. And without controversy great is the mystery of godliness. God was manifest in the flesh.

6. *Jesus Christ will continue to be God and man for ever.* Heb. vii. 24. But this man, because he continueth ever, hath an unchangeable priesthood.

10. *How did Christ, being the Son of God, become man?*

Christ, the Son of God, became man, by taking to himself a *true body*, and *a reasonable soul*, being *conceived* by the power of *the Holy Ghost* in the womb of the Virgin Mary, and was born of her, *yet without sin.*

1. *Christ the Son of God became man.* John i. 14. The Word was made flesh, and dwelt among us.

2. *Christ took to himself a true body.* Heb. ii. 14. Forasmuch then as the children are partakers of flesh and blood, he also himself likewise took part of the same.

3. *Christ took to himself a reasonable soul.* Matt. xxvi. 38. My soul is exceeding sorrowful, even unto death.

4. *Christ was conceived by the power of the Holy Ghost.* Luke i. 35. The Holy Ghost shall come upon thee, and the power of the highest shall overshadow thee.

5. *Christ was born of the Virgin Mary.* Luke ii. 7. And she brought forth her first born son, and wrapped him in swaddling clothes, and laid him in a manger.

6. *Christ was born, and continued to be without sin.* Heb. iv. 15. But was in all points tempted like as we are, yet without sin.

11. *Why did the Son of God become man?*

---

9. *The Redeemer of Man,* The person appointed to buy man back by paying the debt which he had incurred. *Eternal Son of God,* Son of God from eternity. *Glorious Trinity,* Godhead. *Distinct,* Separate. *Person,* Individual.

10. *True body,* Real body, composed of flesh and bones. *A reasonable soul,* A soul possessing all the reasoning faculties of man. *Conceived,* Brought into existence. *The Holy Ghost,* The third person in the Trinity. *Yet without sin,* Completely free from sin.

Christ became man that he might be *an example* of [per]fect *holiness*, teach us *his heavenly doctrine*, and *suffer* die in our room and stead.

1. *Christ became man that he might be an example of perfect [holi]ness.* John xiii. 15. For I have given you an example that ye sh[ould] do as I have done to you.

2. *Christ became man that he might teach us his heavenly doct[rine].* John xv. 15. All things that I have heard of my Father I have m[ade] known unto you.

3. *Christ became man that he might suffer and die in our room [and] stead.* 1 Pet. iii. 18. Christ also hath once suffered for sins, the [just] for the unjust, that he might bring us to God.

12. *Wherein did Christ's humiliation consist?*

Christ's humiliation *consisted* in his being born [of a] woman, in the *meanness* and *poverty* of his *outward* circ[um]stances, in his being forty days *tempted* of the devil, in [his] being *despised* and *rejected of* men, in his *enduring* [the] *cursed death of the cross*, and in his being buried, and [con]tinuing under the power of death for *a time.*

1. *Christ was born of a woman.* Gal. iv. 4. God sent forth his [Son] made of a woman, made under the law.

2. *The outward circumstances of Christ were mean and poor.* M[att.] viii. 20. The foxes have holes, and the birds of the air have n[ests;] but the Son of man hath not where to lay his head.

3. *Christ was forty days tempted of the devil.* Luke iv. 2. B[eing] forty days tempted of the devil.

4. *Christ was despised and rejected of men.* Isa. liii. 3. H[e is] despised and rejected of men, a man of sorrows, and acquainted [with] grief.

5. *Christ endured the cursed death of the cross.* Phil. ii. 8. [He] humbled himself, and became obedient unto death, even the dea[th of] the cross.

6. *Christ was buried, and continued under the power of death [for a]* *time.* Luke xxiii. 53. He took it down, and wrapped it in linen, [and] laid it in a sepulchre that was hewn in stone.

13. *Why did Christ suffer death?*

Christ, by suffering death, made a *full* satisfaction [and] *atonement* to *divine justice* for the *sins of the whole world.*

---

11. *Christ,* The anointed of God. *An example,* A pattern. *Holiness,* Pur[ity of] motive and conduct. *His heavenly doctrine,* Those precepts which are now [con]tained in the New Testament. *Suffer,* Submit to pains and privations.

12. *Consisted,* Lay, or appeared. *Meanness,* Obscurity. *Poverty,* Indig[ence.] *Outward,* Temporal. *Tempted,* Tried. *Despised,* Treated contemptuously. *[Re]jected of,* Considered unworthy of credit by. *Enduring,* Submitting to. *C[ursed,]* Shameful. *Death of the cross,* Suffering of death by being nailed naked to [a cross.] *Continuing,* Remaining. *A time,* A period of three days.

13. *Full,* Complete. *Atonement,* Compensation. *Divine justice,* The infle[xible] and equitable perfection of God. *Sins,* Transgressions and failings. *The [whole] world,* All mankind, without exception, who have lived, who now live, and [who] shall live, to the end of time.

1. *Christ suffered death.* Phil. ii. 8. He became obedient unto death, even the death of the cross.

2. *Christ, by suffering death, made a full satisfaction to divine justice for sin.* Heb. vii. 27. Who needeth not daily, as those high priests, to offer up sacrifice first for his own sins, and then for the people's; for this he did once when he offered up himself.

3. *Christ, by suffering death, made a full atonement for sin.* Heb. x. 14. For by one offering he hath perfected for ever them that are sanctified.

4. *By the death of Christ, satisfaction and atonement were made for the sins of the whole world.* 1 John ii. 2. He is the propitiation for our sins; and not for ours only, but also for the sins of the whole world.

14. *How did the death of Christ satisfy divine justice?*

Our sins *deserved death;* but Christ being both God and man, and *perfectly righteous,* there was an *infinite* value and merit in his death, which being *undergone for our sakes,* and in our *stead,* Almighty God exercises his *mercy in the forgiveness of sins,* consistently with *his justice and holiness.*

1. *Our sins deserved death.* Ezek. xviii. 4. The soul that sinneth it shall die.

2. *Christ was both God and man.* 1 Tim. iii. 16. And without controversy, great is the mystery of godliness. God was manifest in the flesh.

3. *Christ was perfectly righteous.* Heb. vii. 26. For such an high priest became us, who is holy, harmless, undefiled, separate from sinners.

4. *In the death of Christ there was an infinite value and merit.* 1 Pet. i. 18, 19. Ye were not redeemed with corruptible things, as silver and gold—but with the precious blood of Christ, as of a lamb without blemish and without spot.

5. *The death of Christ was undergone for our sakes.* Isa. liii. 5. He was wounded for our transgressions, he was bruised for our iniquities.

6. *The death of Christ was undergone in our stead.* 1 Pet. iii. 18. Christ also hath once suffered for sins, the just for the unjust, that he might bring us to God.

7. *It is through the mercy of Almighty God that sin is forgiven.* Tit. iii. 5. Not by works of righteousness which we have done, but according to his mercy he saved us.

8. *God, in forgiving sins through Christ, acts consistently with his justice and holiness.* Rom. iii. 26. That he might be just, and the justifier of him which believeth in Jesus.

15. *Wherein consisteth Christ's exaltation?*

Christ's exaltation *consisteth in* his rising again from the *dead* on the *third day,* in his *ascending* into heaven, and his

14. *Deserved death,* Merited and rendered us liable to eternal punishment. *Perfectly righteous,* Completely holy. *Infinite,* Unspeakable and unlimited. *Undergone, Sustained. For our sakes,* From love to us. *Stead,* Place. *Mercy,* Disposition to forgive. *In the forgiveness of sins,* In pardoning offences against his person and government. *Consistently,* In perfect accordance. *His justice and holiness,* The inflexible rectitude and purity of his character.

15. *Consisteth in,* Is constituted by. *Dead,* State of death, and coming out of the grave. *Third day,* Third day after his death and burial. *Ascending,* Going up

sitting *at the right hand of God the Father*, and
appointment to *judge the world* at the *last day*.

1. *Christ rose from the dead on the third day.* 1 Cor. xv
rose again the third day according to the scriptures.

2. *Christ ascended into heaven.* Luke xxiv. 51. While he
them, he was parted from them, and carried up into heaven.

3. *Christ is now seated at the right hand of God the Father*
iii. 1. Seek those things which are above, where Christ sitteth
right hand of God.

4. *Christ is appointed to judge the world at the last day.* Ac
31. He hath appointed a day in the which he will judge th
in righteousness by that man whom he hath ordained ; whe
hath given assurance unto all men in that he hath raised hi
the dead.

16. *What offices doth Christ execute as our Redeem*
Christ, as our Redeemer, *executeth the offices of a pr*
of *a priest*, and of *a king*, both in his estate of *humi*
and of *exaltation*.

1. *Christ, as our Redeemer, executes the office of a prophet.*
vi. 14. This is of a truth that prophet that should come in
world.

2. *Christ, as our Redeemer, executes the office of a priest.*
cx. 4. Thou art a priest for ever after the order of Melchisedec

3. *Christ, as our Redeemer, executes the office of a king.* Ma
5. Tell ye the daughter of Zion, Behold thy king cometh un
meek, and sitting upon an ass, and a colt the foal of an ass.

4. *Christ, as our Redeemer, executes these offices in his es*
humiliation. Heb. ix. 28. Christ was once offered to bear the
many.

5. *Christ, as our Redeemer, executes these offices in his estate*
altation. Acts ii. 33. Therefore being by the right hand
exalted, and having received of the Father the promise of th
Ghost, he hath shed forth this which ye now see and hear.

17. *How doth Christ execute the office of a prophet*
Christ executeth the office of a prophet in *revealing*
by his *word* and *spirit*, the *will* of God for our *salvatio*

1. *Christ, as our prophet, makes known to us the will of God.*
xv. 15. All things that I have heard of my Father I have
known unto you.

2. *Christ by his word reveals to us the will of God.* 2 Cor.
God was in Christ reconciling the world unto himself, not im

At the right hand of God the Father, In the highest seat of honour and
Appointment, Being commissioned and directed. *Judge*, Try the cond
character, and to pass sentence upon. *The world*, All men. *Last day,*
judgment.

16. *Christ*, The anointed of God. *Executeth*, Discharges or performs. O
Works or duties belonging to. *A prophet*, One who makes known the will
A priest, One who offers sacrifice, presents its blood, and makes supplie
the people. *A king*, One who rules and protects his subjects. *Humiliation,*
ness and debasement. *Exaltation*, Honour and preferment.

17. *Revealing*, Making known. *His word*, The Bible. *Spirit*, The gra
fluences and workings of the Holy Spirit. *Will*, Intentions. *Salvation,*
ance from the power, pollution, and consequences of sin.

their trespasses unto them, and hath committed unto us the word of reconciliation.

3. *Christ by his Spirit reveals to us the will of God.* John xiv. 26 But the Comforter, which is the Holy Ghost, whom the Father will send in my name, he shall teach you all things.

4. *Christ reveals to us the will of God for our salvation.* John xx. 31. These are written that ye might believe that Jesus is the Christ the Son of God; and that believing ye might have life through his name.

18. *How doth Christ execute the office of a priest ?*

Christ executeth the office of a priest in his once offering up of himself as a sacrifice to satisfy divine justice, and to reconcile us to God, and in making continual intercession for us.

1. *Christ as a priest once offered up himself, a sacrifice.* Heb vii. 27. This he did once when he offered up himself.

2. *Christ as a priest offered up himself to satisfy divine justice.* 1 John ii. 2. He is the propitiation for our sins.

3. *Christ as a priest offered up himself to reconcile us to God.* Eph. ii. 16. That he might reconcile both unto God in one body by the cross, having slain the enmity thereby.

4. *Christ as a priest makes continual intercession.* Heb. vii. 25. He ever liveth to make intercession for them.

19. *How doth Christ execute the office of a king ?*

Christ executeth the office of a king in subduing us to himself, in ruling and defending us, and in restraining and conquering all his and our enemies.

1. *Christ as a king subdues us to himself.* Psalm cx. 3. Thy people shall be willing in the day of thy power.

2. *Christ as a king rules us.* Isa. xxxiii. 22. The Lord is our king, he will save us.

3. *Christ as a king defends us.* Psalm lxxxix. 18. The Lord is our defence, and the holy one of Israel is our king.

4. *Christ as a king restrains all his and our enemies.* Psalm lxxvi. 10. The wrath of man shall praise thee; the remainder of wrath shalt thou restrain.

5. *Christ as a king conquers all his and our enemies.* 1 Cor. xv. 25. He must reign till he hath put all enemies under his feet.

20. *Who were the apostles of our Lord ?*

The apostles of our Lord were twelve men whom he called from among his disciples to be witnesses of his miracles and

18. *Offering up of himself as a sacrifice,* Giving himself freely to suffer death, and the punishment of sin, in the place of sinners. *Satisfy divine justice,* Pay fully the just and righteous demands of God's justice. *Reconcile us,* Make us at peace with; and willing to submit. *Making,* Presenting. *Continual,* Unremitting. *Intercession* Prayers to God.

19. *Subduing us,* Overcoming, conquering, and making us subject. *Ruling,* Guiding or governing. *Defending us,* Preserving us from being injured or hurt. *Restraining,* Keeping in awe, preventing. *Conquering,* Overpowering or destroy.

20. *Called,* Selected and set apart. *Disciples,* Scholars or followers. *Witnesses,* Spectators. *His miracles,* The things which he performed, out of, or opposed to

B

death, resurrection and *ascension,* and wh
timony of *these things,* and to *preach*
Jews and *Gentiles.*

1. *The twelve apostles were called by Jesus C*
disciples. Mark. iii. 14. And he ordained twe
be with him, and that he might send them forth

2. *The apostles were called to be witnesses of th*
Acts. xxii. 15. For thou shalt be his witness t
thou hast seen and heard.

3. *The apostles were called to be witnesses of*
1 Pet. v. 1. The elders which are among you I
an elder, and a witness of the sufferings of Christ

4. *The apostles were called to be witnesses of*
Christ. Mark xvi. 14. Afterward he appeared
they sat at meat, and upbraided them with thei
ness of heart, because they believed not them
after he was risen.

5. *The apostles were called to be witnesses of the*
Luke xxiv. 51. And it came to pass while he b
parted from them, and carried up into heaven.

6. *The apostles were required to bear testimony o*
Acts. i. 8. And ye shall be witnesses unto me, both
all Judea, and in Samaria, and unto the uttermo

7. *The apostles were to preach the gospel to the*
19. Go ye therefore and teach all nations, baptizir
of the Father, and of the Son, and of the Holy G

8. *The apostles were to preach the gospel to th*
34, 35. Then Peter opened his mouth and said, (
that God is no respecter of persons: but in every na
him, and worketh righteousness, is accepted with I

21. *What is the Gospel?*

The Gospel is *an account* of the *comin*
into the world, of *his teaching, his manner*
racles, his death, and his resurrection. *It c*
mands of God to all men *everywhere* to *repe*
and to *believe in Christ.* It is the *promise*
don, sanctify, and save from *eternal death,* a
repent and believe on his Son.

---

the ordinary course of nature. *Death,* His crucifixion and d
His being again alive after having been dead and buried. *As*
into heaven. *Bear testimony,* Give evidence. *These things,*
resurrection, and ascension. *Preach,* Announce and proclaim
of salvation through a Redeemer. *Jews,* Inhabitants of the
descendants of Abraham. *Gentiles,* The people of all the oth
of the earth.

21. *An account,* A narrative. *Coming,* Entrance. *His tea*
in which he instructed his followers. *His manner of life,*
conducted himself in all the different relations and circumsta
ances. *Everywhere,* In whatever place or circumstances. *R*
and forsake. *Sins,* Transgressions of, or disobedience to the c
Christ, Receive and acknowledge Christ as their lawgiver and
Assurance. *Pardon,* Forgive. *Sanctify,* Deliver from the po
nal death, Never-ending misery.

1. *The gospel gives an account of the coming of Christ into the world.* Luke. ii. 7. And she brought forth her first-born son, and wrapped him in swaddling clothes, and laid him in a manger.

2. *The gospel gives an account of the teaching of Christ.* Matt. v. 1. And he opened his mouth and taught them, saying, &c.

3. *The gospel gives an account of Christ's manner of life.* Matt. iv. 23. And Jesus went about all Galilee, teaching in their synagogues, and preaching the gospel of the kingdom, and healing all manner of sickness, and all manner of disease among the people.

4. *The gospel gives an account of Christ's miracles.* Matt. viii. 26. Then he arose and rebuked the winds and the sea; and there was a great calm.

5. *The gospel gives an account of the death of Christ.* Matt. xxvii. 35. And they crucified him.

6. *The gospel gives an account of the resurrection of Christ.* Mark xvi. 9. Now when Jesus was risen early, the first day of the week, he appeared first to Mary Magdalene, out of whom he had cast seven devils.

7. *In the gospel God commands all men everywhere to repent of their sins.* Acts xvii. 30. And the times of this ignorance God winked at, but now commandeth all men everywhere to repent.

8. *In the gospel God commands all men everywhere to believe in Christ.* John viii. 24. If ye believe not that I am he, ye shall die in your sins.

9. *In the gospel God promises to pardon all who repent of their sins and believe on his Son.* Acts xvi. 31. Believe on the Lord Jesus Christ, and thou shalt be saved.

10. *In the gospel God promises to sanctify all who repent and believe on his Son.* Mark ix. 23. All things are possible to him that believeth.

11. *In the gospel God promises to save from eternal death all that repent, and believe on his Son.* Mark xvi. 16. He that believeth and is baptized, shall be saved.

22. *What is true repentance?*

True repentance is *a grace* of the Holy Spirit, *whereby a* sinner, *from a sense of his sin,* and *apprehension of the mercy of God in Christ,* doth, *with grief* and *hatred* of his sin, *turn from it to God,* with *full purpose* of, and *endeavour* after *future obedience.*

1. *True repentance is a grace of the Holy Spirit.* Acts xi. 18. Then hath God also to the Gentiles granted repentance unto life.

2. *In true repentance there is a sense of sin.* Psalm li. 4. Against thee, thee only have I sinned, and done this evil in thy sight.

3. *In true repentance there is an apprehension of the mercy of God.* Rom. ii. 4. The goodness of God leadeth thee to repentance.

4. *The mercy of God to the repenting sinner, is exhibited only in Christ.* Rom. iii. 25. Whom God hath set forth to be a propitiation, through faith in his blood.

---

22. *A grace of,* A favour bestowed by. *Whereby,* By which. *A sense of his sin,* An enlightened conviction of the evil nature, the extent and danger of his sin. *Apprehension,* Perception. *Mercy of God in Christ,* Willingness of God to receive sinners coming to him by Christ. *Grief,* Great sorrow. *Hatred,* Dislike and detestation. *Turn from it to God,* Leave the practice of it for the service of God. *Full purpose,* A complete and decided resolution. *Endeavour,* A determined pursuance. *Future obedience,* Subsequent compliance with all the will of God.

5. *In true repentance there is a sincere grief f...*
I was ashamed, yea, even confounded, because ...
of my youth.

6. *In true repentance there is a sincere hatred ...*
31. Then shall ye remember your own evil w...
that were not good, and shall loathe yourselves ...
your iniquities, and for your abominations.

7. *In true repentance the sinner turns from ...*
30. Repent, and turn yourselves from all your ...

8. *In true repentance the sinner turns to Go...*
us search and try our ways, and turn again to th...

9. *In true repentance there is a full purpose ...*
God. Psalm cxix. 59. I thought on my ways ...
unto thy testimonies.

10. *In true repentance there is an anxious e...*
Jer. xxxi. 18. Turn thou me, and I shall be tu...
Lord my God.

23. *What is faith ?*

Faith is a *conviction* of the *truth* and *rea...*
which God has *told* us in the *Bible.* F...
saving grace, whereby we *receive* and *rest* ...
salvation *as he is offered to us in the gosp...*
we are justified.

1. *The Bible is a revelation from God.* 2 Pet. ...
phecy came not in old time by the will of man ; ...
spake as they were moved by the Holy Ghost.

2. *Faith convinces us of the truth and reality ...*
God has revealed in the Bible. Heb. xi. 1. Now ...
of things hoped for, the evidence of things not se...

3. *Faith in Christ is a saving grace.* Rom. v...
justified by faith we have peace with God.

4. *Christ is offered to us in the gospel.* Acts ...
the Lord Jesus Christ and thou shalt be saved.

5. *By faith we receive Christ as he is offered ...*
John i. 12. As many as received him, to them g...
come the sons of God, even to them that believe ...

6. *By faith we rest upon Christ alone for salvati...*
have believed in Jesus Christ, that we might be ...
of Christ, and not by the works of the law.

7. *By faith in Christ we are justified.* Acts x...
this man is preached unto you the forgiveness of ...
that believe are justified from all things from w...
justified by the law of Moses.

24. *What is justification ?*

23. *Conviction,* Satisfactory persuasion. *Truth,* Authen...
existence. *Told,* Revealed and made known to. *Bible,* Bo...
Testaments. *Saving grace,* Favour bestowed upon us by ...
cessary to our salvation. *Whereby,* By which faith. *Recei...*
Repose and confide in. *Alone,* Only. *Salvation,* Complet...
and restoration to happiness and the friendship of God. ...
in the way and manner in which he is presented. To u...
The gospel, The plan of salvation contained in the Bible. ...
in Christ.

Justification is an act of God's free grace, wherein he pardoneth all our sins, and accepteth us as righteous in his sight, only for the sake of Christ, and at the same time we receive the benefits of adoption and regeneration.

1. Justification is an act of God's free grace. Eph. i. 7. In whom we have redemption through his blood, the forgiveness of sins, according to the riches of his grace.

2. All our sins are pardoned in justification. Jer. xxxiii. 8. I will pardon all their iniquities whereby they have sinned, and whereby they have transgressed against me.

3. In justification we are accepted as righteous in the sight of God. 2 Cor. v. 21. For he hath made him to be sin for us, who knew no sin, that we might be made the righteousness of God in him.

4. We are pardoned and accepted only for the sake of Christ. Gal. ii. 16. Even we have believed in Jesus Christ, that we might be justified by the faith of Christ.

5. At the moment of justification we receive the benefit of adoption. Gal. iv. 7. Wherefore thou art no more a servant but a son, and if a son, then an heir of God through Christ.

6. At the moment of justification we receive the benefit of regeneration. Rom. viii. 1. There is therefore now no condemnation to them which are in Christ Jesus, who walk not after the flesh, but after the Spirit.

25. What is adoption?

Adoption is an act of God's free grace, whereby we are received into the number, and have a right to all the privileges of the sons of God.

1. Adoption is an act of God's free grace. 1 John iii. 1. Behold what manner of love the Father hath bestowed upon us, that we should be called the sons of God.

2. By adoption we are received into the number of the sons of God. John i. 12. As many as received him, to them gave he power to become the sons of God.

3. By adoption we obtain a right to all the privileges of the sons of God. Rom. viii. 17. And if children, then heirs; heirs of God, and joint heirs with Christ.

26. What blessings do in this life accompany our justification and adoption?

The blessings which in this life accompany our justification and adoption, are a sense of God's love, peace of

---

24. An act, A single operation. Grace, Favour and mercy to men. Wherein, In which. Accepteth us, Receiveth us with affection and kindness. Righteous, Free from all blame. The same time, The instant in which we are justified. Benefits, Blessings.

25. Whereby, By which. Right, Just claim. Privileges, Blessings and advantages.

26. Blessings, Spiritual privileges. This life, Our present state of existence. Accompany, Are invariably associated with. A sense of God's love, A heartfelt satisfactory assurance that we are loved by God. Peace of conscience, Repose from

conscience, joy in the Holy Ghost, and h
God.

1. *A present sense of God's love accompanies*
adoption. 2 Cor. v. 1. For we know that if
this tabernacle were dissolved, we have a buildi
not made with hands, eternal in the heavens.

2. *Present peace of conscience accompanies*
adoption. Rom. v. 1. Being justified by faith,
God, through our Lord Jesus Christ.

3. *Present joy in the Holy Ghost accompanies*
adoption. Rom. viii. 16. The Spirit itself bea
spirit, that we are the children of God.

4. *Present hope of the glory of God accompa*
and adoption. 1 John iii. 2. Beloved, now are
and it doth not yet appear what we shall be; but
he shall appear we shall be like him, for we shal

27. *What is regeneration, or the new bir*
Regeneration, or the new birth, is that g
Almighty God *works* in the *whole soul,*
from the *death of sin* to a *life of righte*
creates it anew in Christ Jesus, and when
the *image* of God in *righteousness* and *true*

1. *Regeneration is effected in the soul by Alm*
5. Not by works of righteousness which we have
to his mercy he saved us by the washing of regen
ing of the Holy Ghost.

2. *By regeneration the soul is raised from the*
3. 1. You hath he quickened who were dead in tr

3. *By regeneration the soul is raised to a li*
1 John ii. 29. Ye know that every one that doe
born of him.

4. *By regeneration the soul is created anew in Ch*
v. 17. Therefore if any man be in Christ, he is a
things are passed away, behold, all things are beco

5. *By regeneration the soul is renewed after th*
righteousness and true holiness. Eph. iv. 24. A
the new man, which after God is created in right
.oliness.

28. *What follows from our regeneration*
again?

the painful accusations of the judging moral principle within
Ghost, Happiness in being subjected to the dominion of the I
reigns in the heart. *Hope of the glory of God,* A delightful
fidence of being admitted at last into the realms of eternal feli
27. *Great change,* Important alteration. *Works,* Effects. *W*
intellectual principle by which man is distinguished from
Isaac, Exalts. *Death of sin,* State of moral darkness, degrad
lity to which it is subjected by the transgression of our first re
teousness, State of spiritual light and vigour, in which it labo
conformity to the divine will. *Creates it anew in Christ Je*
branch into Christ, as the vine from whom it afterwards recei
ment. *Renewed after,* Fashioned into. *Image,* Resembla
Moral rectitude. *True holiness,* Freedom from all the defilen

In regeneration our sanctification is begun, and we receive power to *grow in grace*, and in *the knowledge of Christ*, and to live in the *exercise of inward and outward holiness*.

1. *Sanctification begins in regeneration.* 1 Pet. ii. 2. As new-born babes desire the sincere milk of the word, that ye may grow thereby.

2. *When regenerated, we receive power to grow in grace.* Col. i. 11. Strengthened with all might according to his glorious power, unto all patience and long-suffering with joyfulness.

3. *When regenerated, we receive power to grow in the knowledge of Christ.* 2 Pet. iii. 18. Grow in grace, and in the knowledge of our Lord and Saviour Jesus Christ.

4. *When regenerated, we are enabled to live in the exercise of inward holiness.* 2 Thess. ii. 13. God hath from the beginning chosen you to salvation through sanctification of the Spirit.

5. *When regenerated, we are enabled to live in the exercise of outward holiness.* 1 John iii. 3. Every man that hath this hope in him, purifieth himself, even as he is pure.

29. *What is entire sanctification?*

Entire sanctification is the state of being *entirely cleansed* from *sin*, so as to love God with all our *heart*, and *mind*, and *soul*, and *strength*, and *our neighbour as ourselves*.

1. *To be sanctified, is to be entirely cleansed from sin.* Heb. xii. 14. Follow peace with all men, and holiness, without which no man shall see the Lord.

2. *Entire sanctification consists in loving God with all our heart, and mind, and soul, and strength, and our neighbour as ourselves.* Matt. xxii. 37–39. Thou shalt love the Lord thy God with all thy heart, and with all thy soul, and with all thy mind. This is the first and great commandment. And the second is like unto it, Thou shalt love thy neighbour as thyself.

30. *What benefits do believers receive from Christ at death?*

The *souls* of *believers* at death do immediately *pass* into *glory*, and their bodies rest in their graves till *the resurrection*.

1. *The souls of believers at death do immediately pass into glory.* Luke xxiii. 43. Jesus said unto him, Verily I say unto thee, To-day shalt thou be with me in paradise.

---

28. *Power*, Ability. *Grow in grace*, Increase in all the virtues which adorn the man of God. *The knowledge of Christ*, A knowledge of the duties to which we are called, and the privileges we enjoy as Christians. *Exercise*, Enjoyment and practice. *Inward and outward holiness*, Internal purity of intention and desire, and external purity of words and actions.

29. *Entirely*, Completely. *Cleansed*, Purified. *Sin*, Moral and spiritual defilement. *Heart*, Affections. *Mind*, The inclinations of our will. *Soul*, The powers of our mind. *Strength*, All the exertion and perseverance of which we are capable. *Our neighbour*, To love all mankind. *As ourselves*, As we love ourselves.

30. *Souls*, Immaterial and immortal spirits. *Believers*, Those who believe in Jesus Chirst, and serve him upon earth. *Pass*, Remove from this world. *Glory*, The brightness and happiness of heaven. *The resurrection*, The last day, when all the dead shall be again raised to life.

2. *The bodies of believers rest in their graves*
Isa. lvii. 2. They shall rest in their beds, each o:
rightness.

31. *What benefits will believers receive f*
resurrection?

At the resurrection, believers being *ra*
shall be *openly acknowledged and accepte*
judgment, and made *perfectly blessed* in t:
of God to all eternity.

1. *At the resurrection, believers shall be raised*
xv. 43. It is sown in dishonour, it is raised in glor
2. *Believers shall be openly acknowledged by C*
judgment. Matt. x. 32. Whosoever therefore sha
men, him will I confess also before my Father wl
3. *Believers shall be openly accepted by Christ*
ment. Matt. xxv. 34. Come ye blessed of my
kingdom prepared for you from the foundation o:
4. *Believers shall be made perfectly blessed in th*
God. 1 Cor. ii. 9. Eye hath not seen, nor ear h
entered into the heart of man, the things which Go
them that love him.
5. *Believers shall enjoy God through all eternity*
So shall we ever be with the Lord.

32. *Who is the Holy Ghost ?*

The Holy Ghost is the third *person* in t:
in power and glory to the Father and the S
creation moved upon the face of the water
different kinds of animals are preserved fron
whom the *writers of the Holy Scriptures* we:
framed the human nature of Christ in the w
gin, so that he was born *without sin*, and w
wisdom and *grace without measure.*

---

31. *Raised up*, Brought up out of their graves. *Glory*, Grea:
splendour. *Openly acknowledged and accepted*, Owned by Go:
children before the whole world. *Day of judgment*, Day
Christ will judge all mankind. *Perfectly blessed*, Completel:
ment of God, Possession of the love and gracious presence of :
Time without end.

32. *Person*, Distinct and separate individual. *The trinity*,
Godhead. *Equal*, Exactly alike. *In the creation*, When all
into existence. *Moved upon the face of the waters*, Reduced int:
which were held in solution by, floated in, or were sunk unde:
ent kinds, Various species and tribes. *Animals*, Sentient co:
served, Kept in existence. *Age to Age*, One generation to :
Persons who composed and dictated. *Holy Scriptures*, Books
Testaments. *Inspired*, Disposed and directed. *Framed*, Co:
The Virgin, A young woman called Mary, prior to her becomi:
Without sin, Free from that moral defilement to which all me
ject. *Wisdom*, Knowledge. *Grace*, All spiritual gifts. *Wi*
amount which can neither be measured nor calculated.

1. *The Holy Ghost is the third person in the trinity.* 1 John v. 7. For there are three that bear record in heaven, the Father, the Word, and the Holy Ghost.

2. *The Holy Ghost is equal in power and glory to the Father and the Son.* Matt. xxviii. 19. Go ye therefore and teach all nations, baptizing them in the name of the Father, and of the Son, and of the Holy Ghost.

3. *The Holy Ghost in creation moved upon the face of the waters.* Gen. i. 2. The Spirit of God moved upon the face of the waters.

4. *The Holy Ghost preserves the different kinds of animals from age to age.* Psalm civ. 30. Thou sendest forth thy Spirit, they are created; and thou renewest the face of the earth.

5. *The Holy Ghost inspired the writers of the holy Scriptures.* 2 Pet. i. 21. Holy men of God spake as they were moved by the Holy Ghost.

6. *The Holy Ghost framed the human nature of Christ in the womb of the virgin.* Matt. i. 18. Now the birth of Jesus Christ was on this wise: When as his mother Mary was espoused to Joseph, before they came together, she was found with child of the Holy Ghost.

7. *Christ was born without sin.* Luke i. 35. The Holy Ghost shall come upon thee, and the power of the highest shall overshadow thee; therefore also that holy thing which shall be born of thee, shall be called the Son of God.

8. *The Holy Ghost gave to Christ wisdom without measure.* John iii. 34. God giveth not the Spirit by measure unto him.

9. *The Holy Ghost gave to Christ grace without measure.* Luke iv. 18. The Spirit of the Lord is upon me, because he hath anointed me to preach the gospel to the poor, he hath sent me to heal the broken-hearted, to preach deliverance to the captives, and recovering of sight to the blind, to set at liberty them that are bruised.

33. *What offices does the Holy Ghost perform for those who believe in Christ?*

The Holy Ghost *enlightens the minds* of those who believe in Christ to *understand* the *Scriptures*, *assists* them in their *prayers*, *bears witness with their spirits* that they are the children of God, *comforts* them in *trouble*, *sanctifies them from* all *inward and outward sin*, fills their hearts with *perfect* love to God, and to all mankind, and *imparts* to them all other excellent *graces* and *virtues.*

1. *The Holy Ghost enlightens the minds of believers to understand the Scriptures.* John xvi. 13. When he the Spirit of truth is come, he will guide you into all truth.

2. *The Holy Ghost assists believers in their prayers.* Rom. viii. 26. The spirit itself maketh intercession for us with groanings which cannot be uttered.

---

33. *Enlightens the minds,* Illuminates the understandings. *Understand,* Comprehend the spiritual meaning of. *Scriptures,* Holy oracles of God. *Assists,* Helps. *Prayers,* Supplications at the throne of grace. *Bears witness with their spirits,* Joins his evidence to the evidence of their own spirits. *Comforts,* Consoles and supports. *Trouble,* Their afflictions and calamities. *Sanctifies them from,* Frees them from the power of. *Inward and outward sin,* Internal disinclination, and external opposition to the divine will. *Perfect,* Unreserved. *Imparts,* Gives. *Graces,* Spiritual influences. *Virtues,* Moral qualities.

3. *The Holy Ghost bears witness with the spirit*
they are the children of God. Rom. viii. 16. The S
witness with our spirit, that we are the children of

4. *The Holy Ghost comforts believers when th*
John xiv. 26. But the Comforter, which is the Hol
Father will send in my name, he shall teach you a

5. *The Holy Ghost sanctifies believers from all in*
sin. 1 Thess. v. 23. The very God of peace san
and I pray God your whole spirit, and soul, and b
blameless unto the coming of our Lord Jesus Chris

6. *The Holy Ghost fills the hearts of believers w*
God. Gal. iv. 6. Because ye are sons, God hath se
of his Son into your hearts, crying, Abba, Father.

7. *The Holy Ghost fills the hearts of believers w*
all mankind. 1 John iii. 14. We know that we
death unto life, because we love the brethren. F
his brother abideth in death.

8. *All excellent gifts and graces which believers pos*
the Holy Ghost. Gal. v. 22, 23. The fruit of the S
peace, long-suffering, gentleness, goodness, faith,
perance.

34. *What offices doth the Holy Ghost p*
church of Christ?

The Holy Ghost *calls* and *qualifies* men fro
to *preach the word*, and to *administer the sa*
ders their preaching effectual to the *convers*
and to the *edification of believers*, is present i
nances of public worship, and whose *help* and c
obtained by prayer.

1. *The preachers of the gospel are called by the H*
xx. 28. Take heed therefore unto yourselves, and
over the which the Holy Ghost hath made you overs

2. *The preachers of the gospel are qualified by*
Zech. iv. 6. Not by might nor by power, but by my
Lord of Hosts.

3. *The preached word is rendered effectual to the co*
ners by the Holy Ghost. 1 Thess. i. 5. Our gospel
you in word only, but also in power, and in the Hol
much assurance.

4. *The preached word is rendered effectual to the e*
lievers by the Holy Ghost. Eph. iii. 16, 17. To be str
might by his Spirit in the inner man, that Christ ma
hearts by faith.

5. *The Holy Ghost is present in all the ordinances*

34. *Calls*, By secret suggestions and influences, disposes. Q
and graces enables. *Preach the word*, Explain and enforce
tained in the Scriptures. *Administer the Sacraments*, Dispense
nances of Baptism and the Lord's Supper. *Renders*, Makes.
The serious addresses which they deliver to the people. *Effe*
powerful. *Conversion of sinners*, Deliverance of the ungodly from
Satan into the glorious liberty of the sons of God. *Edification of*
mation and improvement of those who have already received Chris
Ordinances of public worship, Assemblies of God's people in the
Assistance. *Comfort*, Consolation and support. *Obtained*, Had o

ship. Matt. xviii. 20. For where two or three are gathered together in my name, there am I in the midst of them.

6. *The help of the Holy Ghost may be obtained by prayer.* Luke xi. 13. If ye then, being evil, know how to give good gifts unto your children, how much more shall your heavenly Father give the Holy Spirit to them that ask him.

7. *The comfort of the Holy Ghost may be obtained by prayer.* Matt. xxi. 22. And all things whatsoever ye shall ask in prayer, believing, ye shall receive.

35. *What is the law of God?*

The law of God, which is to be found in the Holy Scriptures, is his *will respecting mankind*, both as to what they are to do, and what they are *to leave undone :* this law is *holy*, and *just*, and *good ;* and Jesus Christ has *declared*, that it is *comprehended* in loving God with all our heart, and with all our soul, and with all our mind, and *our neighbour as ourselves*.

1. *The law of God is contained in the holy Scriptures.* 2 Tim. iii. 16. All scripture is given by inspiration of God, and is profitable for doctrine, for reproof, for correction, for instruction in righteousness.

2. *In the Scriptures, mankind are informed what God wills them to do.* John xx. 31. These are written that ye might believe that Jesus is the Christ, the Son of God, and that believing ye might have life through his name.

3. *In the Scriptures, mankind are informed what God wills them to leave undone.* 2 Tim. ii. 19. Let every one that nameth the name of Christ, depart from iniquity.

4. *The law of God is holy.* Rom. vii. 12. Wherefore the law is holy, and the commandment holy, and just, and good.

5. *The law of God is just.* Psalm xix. 7. The law of the Lord is perfect, converting the soul.

6. *The law of God is good.* 1 Tim. i. 8. We know that the law is good.

7. *Christ has declared that the law of God is comprehended in loving God with all our heart, and with all our soul, and with all our mind, and our neighbour as ourselves.* Matt. xxii. 37—40.

36. *Have we not a larger summary of the law of God also in the Scriptures?*

We have a *larger summary* of the *law of God* in the Ten Commandments, *first written* by the finger of God on two *tables* of stone, and *given to Moses*, but now *recorded* in the twentieth chapter of the book of Exodus.

---

35. *Will*, Wish or desire. *Respecting*, With regard to. *Mankind*, The human race. *To leave undone*, Not to do. *Holy*, free from every impure tendency. *Just*, Equitable in all its demands. *Good*, Exactly suitable to man's circumstances. *Declared*, Given us to understand in the plainest terms. *Comprehended*, Summed up. *Our neighbour as ourselves*, Loving our neighbour to the same degree as we love ourselves.

36. *Larger summary*, More extended compendium. *Law of God*, Rule which God has given for the government of mankind. *First*, Originally. *Written*, Marked out in legible characters. *Tables*, Flat pieces. *Given to*, Committed to the care of. *Recorded*, written or printed.

1. *The ten commandments are a larger summa*
vii. 19. Did not Moses give you the law? and ye
the law.

2. *The ten commandments were first written b*
two tables of stone. Exod. xxxi. 18. And he ga
he had made an end of communing with him u
tables of testimony, tables of stone, written wit

3. *The two tables of stone on which God hath*
mandments, were given to Moses. Exod. xx
turned and went down from the mount, and t
testimony were in his hand.

4. *The ten commandments, which were first wr*
God on two tables of stone, are now recorded in
of the book of Exodus. (See Exod. xx.)

37. *Have these Ten Commandments any*

The Ten Commandments are called the
in substance contain all the *moral duties re*
kind, in the Scriptures. And they are *al*
law, to *distinguish them from the laws gi*
children of Israel, respecting the ceremonie
worship, and their political duties, which
ing upon the Israelites only.

1. *The ten commandments are called the moral*

2. *The ten commandments are called the moral*
substance contain all the moral duties required o
Scriptures.

3. *The ten commandments are called the mora*
them from the ceremonial and political laws which
dren of Israel.

4. *The laws which God gave to the children of*
ceremonies of their religious worship, were chie
Israelites only. Eph. ii. 15. Having abolished in
even the law of commandments contained in ordi

4. *The laws which God gave to the children*
their political duties, were chiefly binding upon th

38. *Which is the first commandment ?*

The first commandment is, Thou shalt h
but me.

39. *Which is the second commandment ?*

The second commandment is, Thou shal

---

37. *In substance,* Embody, and in their essence. *Cont*
duties, Virtuous practices. *Required of,* Commanded by G
Also, For this other reason. *Called,* Denominated. *Distingu*
them from being associated with. *Laws,* Rules and reg
Israel, Descendants of the patriarch Jacob, whose name (
Respecting, With reference to. *Ceremonies,* External forms
ship, The ordinances appointed by God to be observed in th
under that dispensation. *Their political duties,* The dutie
called with regard to the civil or earthly government und
Chiefly, Principally. *Binding upon,* Necessary to be observe
38. *But me,* Except me, or in my presence or sight.

thee any *graven image*, nor the likeness of any thing that is in heaven above, or in the earth beneath, or in the water under the earth.   Thou shalt not bow down thyself to them, nor *worship them*, for I the Lord thy God am *a jealous God*, and *visit* the *sins* of the fathers upon the children unto the *third and fourth generation* of them that hate me, and *shew mercy* unto thousands in them that love me and keep my commandments.

40. *Which is the third commandment ?*

The third commandment is, Thou shalt not *take the name of* the Lord thy God *in vain*, for the Lord will not hold him *guiltless* that taketh his name in vain.

41. *Which is fourth commandment ?*

The fourth commandment is, *Remember* that thou *keep holy* the *Sabbath-day*.   Six days shalt thou *labour*, and do all that thou hast to do, but the seventh day is the Sabbath of the Lord thy God ; in it thou shalt do no manner of work, thou, and thy son, and thy daughter, thy man-servant, and thy maid-servant, thy cattle, and *the stranger* that is within thy *gates.*   For in six days the Lord made heaven and earth, the sea, and *all that in them is*, and rested the seventh day ; *wherefore* the Lord blessed the seventh day, and *hallowed it.*

42. *Which is the fifth commandment ?*

The fifth commandment is, *Honour* thy father and thy mother, that thy days may be *long* in the land which the Lord thy God giveth thee.

43. *Which is the sixth commandment ?*

The sixth commandment is, Thou shalt *do no murder.*

---

39. *Graven image*, Hewn, cut, or carved representation. *Worship them*, Perform the ceremonies which may belong to their worship. *A jealous God*, A God exceedingly watchful and suspicious in any thing relating to my worship. *Visit*, Inflict the punishment due to. *Sins*, Transgressions and disobedience. *Third and fourth generation*, Grand-children, and great-grand-children. *Shew mercy*, Exhibit forgiveness and kindness.

40. *Take the name of*, Utter or use those peculiar titles, works, or attributes, which make known and distinguish from every other being. *In vain*, In a light, irreverent, or improper manner. *Guiltless*, Free from liability to punishment.

41. *Remember*, Keep in mind, do not forget. *Keep holy*, Set apart from other days for holy and religious purposes. *Sabbath-day*, Day of rest. *Labour*, Engage in thy ordinary occupation. *The Stranger*, Any person not belonging to thy family. *Gates*, House. *All that in them is*, Every thing that is in the earth and sea. *Wherefore*. For which reason. *Hallowed it*, Sanctified or made it holy.

42. *Honour*, Love, reverence, obey, and provide for. *Long*, Prosperous, happy, and long continued.

43. *Do no murder*, Not take away human life, or do any thing which may tend to shorten it.

C

44. *Which is the seventh commandment?*

The seventh commandment is, Thou shalt not commit adultery.

45. *Which is the eighth commandment?*

The eighth commandment is, Thou shalt not *steal.*

46. *Which is the ninth commandment?*

The ninth commandment is, Thou shalt not *bear false witness* against thy neighbour.

47. *Which is the tenth commandment?*

The tenth commandment is, Thou shalt not *covet* thy neighbour's house, thou shalt not covet thy neighbour's wife, nor his servant, nor his maid, nor his ox, nor his ass, nor any thing that is his.

48. *What do you learn from the ten commandments with respect to your duty towards God?*

My duty towards God is to *believe in him,* to *fear him,* and to love him with all my heart, with all my mind, with all my soul, and with all my strength ; to *worship him,* to *give him thanks,* to *put my whole trust in him,* to *call upon* him, to *honour* his holy name, his *Sabbath,* and his *word,* and to *serve him truly* all the days of my *life.*

1. *It is our duty to believe in God.* Heb. xi. 6. He that cometh to God must believe that he is, and that he is a rewarder of them that diligently seek him.

2. *It is our duty to fear God.* Eccles. xii. 13. Fear God and keep his commandments, for this is the whole duty of man.

3. *It is our duty to love God with all our heart, and mind, and soul, and strength.* Mark xii. 30. And thou shalt love the Lord thy God with all thy heart, and with all thy soul, and with all thy mind, and with all thy strength.

4. *It is our duty to worship God.* Matt. iv. 10. Thou shalt worship the Lord thy God, and him only shalt thou serve.

5. *It is our duty to give God thanks.* Eph. v. 20. Giving thanks always for all things unto God and the Father, in the name of our Lord Jesus Christ.

6. *It is our duty to put our whole trust in God.* 2 Cor. i. 9. We should not trust in ourselves, but in God which raiseth the dead.

45. *Steal,* Take by theft that which is not thine own.

46. *Bear,* Say or affirm. *False witness,* Any thing contrary to what is the truth.

47. *Covet,* Unlawfully or irregularly desire to possess.

48. *Believe in him,* Have a firm persuasion of his being and perfections. *Fear him,* Regard him with awe and reverence. *Worship him,* Pay him divine honours. *Give him thanks,* Feel and express gratitude to him for all his mercies. *Put my whole trust in him,* Commit with confidence all my concerns to his care. *Call upon,* Pray to. *Honour,* Hold in veneration. *Sabbath,* Day of rest. *Serve him truly,* Devote without reservation to his service the powers of my body and mind. *Life,* Existence in this world.

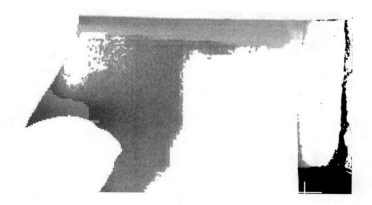

7. *It is our duty to call upon God.* Psalm l. 15. Call upon me in the day of trouble; I will deliver thee, and thou shalt glorify me.

8. *It is our duty to honour God's holy name.* 1 Sam. ii. 30. Them that honour me I will honour, and they that despise me shall be lightly esteemed.

9. *It is our duty to honour God's Sabbath.* Lev. xix. 30. Ye shall keep my sabbaths, and reverence my sanctuary, I am the Lord.

10. *It is our duty to honour God's word.* Isa. lxvi. 2. To this man will I look, even to him that is poor, and of a contrite spirit, and trembleth at my word.

11. *It is our duty to serve God truly all the days of our life.* 1 Chron. xxviii. 9. And thou, Solomon my son, know thou the God of thy Father, and serve him with a perfect heart, and with a willing mind;—if thou seek him, he will be found of thee; but if thou forsake him, he will cast thee off for ever.

49. *What do you learn from the ten commandments with regard to your duty towards your neighbour?* (Part 1st.)

My duty towards my neighbour is to *love him as myself*, and to do to all men as I would *they should do unto me;* to *love, honour,* and *succour* my father and mother; to honour and *obey* the *king,* and all that *are put in authority* under him; to *submit myself to* all my governors, teachers, *spiritual pastors,* and masters; to *order* myself *lowly* and reverently to all my *betters,* and to *hurt nobody* by word or *deed.*

1. *It is my duty to love my neighbour as myself.* Matt. xxii. 39. Thou shalt love thy neighbour as thyself.

2. *It is my duty to do to all men as I would they should do unto me.* Matt. vii. 12. All things whatsoever ye would that men should do to you, do ye even so to them.

3. *It is my duty to love my father and mother.* Mark vii. 10. Whoso curseth father or mother, let him die the death.

4. *It is my duty to honour my father and mother.* Deut. v. 16. Honour thy father and thy mother, as the Lord thy God hath commanded thee.

5. *It is my duty to succour my father and mother.* Gen. xlvii. 12. And Joseph nourished his father, and his brethren, and all his father's household, with bread.

6. *It is my duty to honour the king.* 1 Pet. ii. 17. Honour the king.

7. *It is my duty to obey the king.* 1 Pet. ii. 13. Submit yourself to every ordinance of man for the Lord's sake, whether it be to the king, as supreme.

8. *It is my duty to honour and obey all that are put in authority under the king.* 1 Tim. ii. 1, 2. I exhort therefore, that, first of all

---

49. *Love him as myself,* Be as anxious to promote his welfare as I am to promote my own. *They should do unto me,* Wish them to do to me if I were in their circumstances and they in mine. *Love,* Feel an affection for. *Honour,* To treat with respect and reverence. *Succour,* To assist, and if necessary, supply with the means of comfortable existence. *Obey,* Attend to all the lawful commands of. *King,* Supreme magistrate of the land. *Are put in authority,* Hold official situations. *Submit myself to,* Acquiesce in the authority of. *Spiritual pastors,* Those who are appointed to lead me in the way to heaven. *Order,* Conduct. *Lowly,* Humbly. *Betters,* Superiors. *Hurt nobody,* Do no person harm or injury. *Deed,* Action.

supplications, prayers, intercessions, and giving of thanks, be made for all men. For kings, and for all that are in authority.

9. *It is my duty to submit myself to all my governors.* 1 Pet. ii. 14. Or unto governors, as unto them that are sent by him for the punishment of evil-doers, and for the praise of them that do well.

10. *It is my duty to submit myself to all my teachers.* Rom. xiii. 1 Let every soul be subject unto the higher powers.

11. *It is my duty to submit myself to all my spiritual pastors.* Heb. xiii. 17. Obey them that have the rule over you, and submit yourselves; for they watch for your souls, as they that must give account.

12. *It is my duty to submit myself to all my masters.* 1 Pet. ii. 18. Servants, be subject to your own masters with all fear; not only to the good and gentle, but also to the froward.

13. *It is my duty to order myself lowly to all my betters.* Luke xiv. 11. He that humbleth himself shall be exalted.

14. *It is my duty to order myself reverently to all my betters.* 2 Sam. ix. 6. Now when Mephibosheth, the son of Jonathan, the son of Saul, was come unto David, he fell on his face, and did reverence.

15. *It is my duty to hurt nobody by word.* Tit. iii. 2. Speak evil of no man.

16. *It is my duty to hurt nobody by deed.* Deut. xxvii. 17. Cursed be he that removeth his neighbour's landmark.

50. *What do you learn from the ten commandments with regard to your duty towards your neighbour?* (Part 2nd.)

I learn to be *true* and *just* in all my *dealings;* to bear no *malice* nor *hatred* in my heart; to *keep* my hands from *picking* and *stealing,* and my tongue from *evil-speaking, lying* and *slandering;* to *keep* my body in *temperance, soberness,* and *chastity,* not to covet or desire other men's goods, but to *learn* and *labour truly* to get *my own living,* and to do my *duty* in that state of life into which it shall please God *to call me.*

1. *It is my duty to be true and just in all my dealings.* Prov. xi. 1. A false balance is abomination to the Lord.

2. *It is my duty to bear no malice nor hatred in my heart.* Eph. iv. 26. Be ye angry and sin not: let not the sun go down upon your wrath.

3. *It is my duty to keep my hands from picking and stealing.* Exod. xx. 15. Thou shalt not steal.

4. *It is my duty to keep my tongue from evil-speaking.* Tit. iii. 2. Speak evil of no man.

50. *True,* Faithful. *Just,* Upright and equitable. *Dealings,* Transactions of worldly business. *Bear,* Entertain. *Malice,* Desire to hurt. *Hatred,* Ill-will. *Keep,* Prevent or hold. *Picking,* Robbing. *Stealing,* Taking by theft that which belongs to another. *Evil-speaking,* Exposing the faults of others without cause. *Lying,* Stating as true what I know to be false. *Slandering,* Bringing disgrace or an ill name upon the innocent. *Keep,* Preserve. *Temperance,* A state free from the effects of immoderate eating. *Soberness,* Free from the effects of intoxicating liquors. *Chastity,* In a state of continence. *Learn,* Receive instruction with docility. *Labour truly,* Work with fidelity and industry *My own living,* The means wherewith to live. *My duty,* All that devolves upon me. *To call me,* By his providence to direct me.

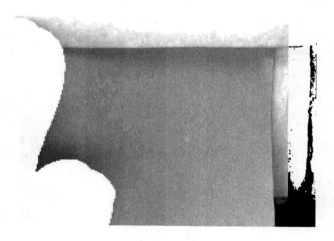

5. *It is my duty to keep my tongue from lying.* Rev. xxi. 8. All liars shall have their part in the lake which burneth with fire and brimstone.

6. *It is my duty to keep my tongue from slandering.* Psalm cl. 5. Whoso privily slandereth his neighbour, him will I cut off.

7. *It is my duty to keep my body in temperance, soberness, and chastity.* 1 Cor. vi. 9, 10. Be not deceived; neither fornicators, nor idolaters, nor adulterers, nor effeminate, nor abusers of themselves with mankind; nor thieves, nor covetous, nor drunkards, nor revilers, nor extortioners, shall inherit the kingdom of God.

8. *I must not covet nor desire other men's goods.* Psalm cxix. 36. Incline my heart unto thy testimonies, and not to covetousness.

9. *I must learn and labour truly to get my own living.* Rom. xii. 17. Provide things honest in the sight of all men.

10. *I must do my duty in that state of life into which it shall please God to call me.* 1 Tim. v. 8. If any provide not for his own, and specially for those of his own house, he hath denied the faith, and is worse than an infidel.

51. *What special instruction has Jesus Christ given us with regard to our duties?*

Jesus Christ has *taught us* to love one another, to *guard* against *sin* in our *thoughts* and *purposes*, as well as in our *outward actions*, to *help* and *relieve* all who are in *distress*, to do to others as we would wish them to do to us, to love *our enemies*, to *forgive* those who have *injured us*, to be *meek* and *lowly*, to be *patient* under *sufferings*, and to be *kind* to all men.

1. *Jesus Christ has taught us to love one another.* John xiii. 35. By this shall all men know that ye are my disciples, if ye have love one to another.

2. *Jesus Christ has taught us that we may not only guard against sin in our outward actions, but also in our thoughts and purposes.* Matt. v. 22. Whosoever is angry with his brother without a cause, shall be in danger of the judgment.

3. *Jesus Christ has taught us to help and relieve all who are in distress.* Matt. xxv. 36. I was sick, and ye visited me.

4. *Jesus Christ has taught us to do to others as we would wish them to do to us.* Matt. vii. 12. Whatsoever ye would that men should do to you, do ye even so to them.

5. *Jesus Christ has taught us to love our enemies.* Matt. v. 44. Love your enemies, bless them that curse you, do good to them that hate you, and pray for them which despitefully use you and persecute you.

6. *Jesus Christ has taught us to forgive those who have injured us.* Matt. vi. 15. If ye forgive not men their trespasses, neither will your Father forgive your trespasses.

---

51. *Taught us*, Instructed his followers. *Guard*, Be suspicious of, and watch. *Sin*, Whatever is inconsistent with the purity of God's law. *Thoughts*, Imaginations or inclinations. *Purposes*, Resolutions. *Our outward actions*, The works which we actually perform. *Help*, Assist. *Relieve*, If possible remove the cause of uneasiness from. *Distress*, Afflictions, whether of body or mind. *Our enemies*, Those who hate and try to hurt us. *Forgive*, Pardon. *Injured us*, Done us harm. *Meek*, Mild in our temper. *Lowly*, Humble in our manner. *Patient*, Without fretfulness. *Sufferings*, Pains or privations. *Kind*, Benevolent.

C 2

7. *Jesus Christ has taught us to be meek and lowly.* Matt. xi. 29. Learn of me, for I am meek and lowly in heart.

8. *Jesus Christ has taught us to be patient under suffering.* Luke xxi. 19. In your patience possess ye your souls.

9. *Jesus Christ has taught us to be kind to all men.* Gal. vi. 10. As we have therefore opportunity, let us do good unto all men.

52. *What precepts does the New Testament contain as to our conduct in the different relations of life?*

In the New Testament, husbands are *instructed to love their wives;* wives are to be *submissive to their husbands;* parents are not to *provoke their children,* but *to train them up for God;* children are to be *obedient to* their *parents;* servants are to be *in subjection to their masters;* masters are to give to their servants that which is *just and right;* and we are to be submissive to magistrates, governors, and ministers of the gospel.

1. *In the New Testament, husbands are instructed to love their wives.* Eph. v. 25. Husbands, love your wives, even as Christ also loved the church, and gave himself for it.

2. *In the New Testament, wives are instructed to be submissive to their husbands.* Eph. v. 22. Wives, submit yourselves unto your own husbands, as unto the Lord.

3. *In the New Testament, parents are instructed not to provoke their children, but to train them up for God.* Eph. vi. 4. Fathers, provoke not your children to wrath; but bring them up in the nurture and admonition of the Lord.

4. *In the New Testament, children are instructed to be obedient to their parents.* Eph. vi. 1. Children, obey your parents in the Lord; for this is right.

5. *In the New Testament, servants are instructed to be in subjection to their masters.* 1 Pet. ii. 18. Servants, be subject to your masters with all fear; not only to the good and gentle, but also to the froward.

6. *In the New Testament, masters are instructed to give to their servants that which is just and right.* Col. iv. 1. Masters, give unto your servants that which is just and equal, knowing that ye also have a Master in heaven.

7. *In the New Testament, we are instructed to be submissive to magistrates.* Rom. xiii. 1. Let every soul be subject unto the higher powers; for there is no power but of God: the powers that be are ordained of God.

8. *In the New Testament, we are instructed to be submissive to governors.* 1 Pet. ii. 17. Honour all men. Love the brotherhood. Fear God. Honour the king.

---

52. *Instructed,* Taught and commanded. *Love,* Feel an affection for, and treat with respect and kindness. *Their wives,* The women to whom they are married. *Submissive,* Obedient and subservient. *Their husbands,* The men to whom they are united by marriage. *Provoke their children,* Treat their children in such a way as to excite their anger. *To train them up,* By discipline and doctrine to educate them. *For God,* That they may promote the glory of God. *Obedient to,* Subject to the authority of. *Parents,* Father and mother. *In subjection to,* Under the rule and government of. *Their masters,* The persons under whose authority they, by the providence of God, have been placed. *Just and right,* Equitable and proper

9. *In the New Testament, we are instructed to be submissive to the ministers of the gospel.* Heb. xiii. 17. Obey them that have the rule over you, and submit yourselves; for they watch for your souls, as they that must give account.

53. *To what end serveth the law of God?*

The law of God *serveth* as the rule of our conduct, and to *convince us* of sin.

1. *The law of God serves as the rule of our conduct.* Psalm cxix. 1. Blessed are the undefiled in the way, who walk in the law of the Lord.

2. *The law of God serves to convince us of sin.* Rom. iii. 20. By the law is the knowledge of sin.

54. *Are all transgressions of the law equally great?*

Some sins *in themselves,* and *by reason* of several *aggravations,* are *more heinous* in the sight of God than *others.*

1. *Some sins are in themselves more heinous in the sight of God than others.* John xix. 11. He that delivered me unto thee, hath the greater sin.

2. *Aggravations make sin more heinous in the sight of God.* Matt. xxiii. 14. Woe unto you, Scribes and Pharisees, hypocrites! for ye devour widows' houses, and for a pretence make long prayers; therefore ye shall receive the greater damnation.

55. *What doth every sin deserve?*

Every sin deserveth God's *wrath* and *curse,* both in *this life,* and *that which is to come.*

1. *Every sin deserves the wrath and curse of God in this life.* Gal. iii. 10. Cursed is every one that continueth not in all things which are written in the book of the law to do them.

2. *Every sin deserves the wrath and curse of God in the life that is to come.* Matt. xxv. 41. Then shall he say also unto them on the left hand, Depart from me, ye cursed, into everlasting fire, prepared for the devil and his angels.

56. *Does the law of God promise the pardon of sin to those who have transgressed it?*

The law of God *does not promise pardon* to those who have *transgressed it;* pardon is promised only in the *gospel* through

---

53. *Serveth,* Is of use. *Convince us,* Shew us that we are guilty.

54. *In themselves,* In their own nature. *By reason,* On account. *Several,* Many, different. *Aggravations,* Circumstances accompanying them, which make them still more evil and hateful than they otherwise would be. *More heinous,* Much more wicked and atrocious. *Others,* Other sins which are not so aggravated.

55. *Every sin,* Every single sin which we commit in thought, word, or deed, however trivial it may in itself appear, and although it may not be accompanied with any aggravated circumstances. *Wrath,* Anger. *Curse,* Sentence and infliction of severe punishment. *This life,* This world. *That which is to come,* In the state of being after death.

56. *Does not promise,* Makes no declarations to excite expectations of. *Pardon,* Forgiveness. *Transgressed it.* Violated its precepts. *Gospel,* Scriptural development of that plan which Almighty God devised for the redemption of the world

faith in our Lord Jesus Christ, all, *therefore*, who do not *repent of* their sins, and *believe* in Christ, must *remain for ever under the curse* of the law.

1. *The law of God does not promise pardon to those who have transgressed it.* Gal. ii. 16. Knowing that a man is not justified by the works of the law, but by the faith of Jesus Christ, even we have believed in Jesus Christ, that we might be justified by the faith of Christ.

2. *Pardon is promised only in the gospel.* Isa. lv. 7. Let the wicked forsake his way, and the unrighteous man his thoughts : and let him return unto the Lord, and he will have mercy upon him ; and to our God, for he will abundantly pardon.

3. *The gospel promises pardon through faith in our Lord Jesus Christ.* Mark xvi. 16. He that believeth and is baptized, shall be saved.

4. *All who have not repented of their sins, are under the curse of the law.* Luke xiii. 3. Except ye repent, ye shall all likewise perish.

5. *All who do not believe in Christ are under the curse of the law.* John iii. 18. He that believeth not is condemned already, because he hath not believed in the name of the only begotten Son of God.

6. *All who do not repent of their sins and believe in Christ, must remain for ever under the curse of the law.* Mark xvi. 16. He that believeth not shall be damned.

57. *Might we not obtain the forgiveness of sins by repenting, and keeping the law of God in future?*

Repentance and *amendment of life* cannot *atone for past sin*, nor *satisfy* the justice of God ; but we may obtain **the remission** of sin by *trusting in* the *merits* of Christ, as *helpless*, *guilty*, and *undone sinners ;* and being *regenerated* by the Holy Spirit, we shall be enabled by his *help thenceforward* to please God and keep his commandments.

1. *Repentance and amendment of life cannot atone for past sin.* Rom. viii. 8. They that are in the flesh cannot please God.

2. *Repentance and amendment of life cannot satisfy the justice of God.* Ezek. xviii. 4. The soul that sinneth it shall die.

3. *By trusting in the merits of Christ, we may obtain the remission of sin.* Acts x. 43. Whosoever believeth in him shall receive remission of sins.

4. *We must feel ourselves helpless, guilty, and undone sinners, before we can obtain remission of sin.* Isa. lxvi. 2. To this man will I

---

and of which we obtain the benefit. *Faith*, Believing. *Therefore*, For this reason. *Repent of*, Confess and forsake. *Believe*, Implicitly repose and confide. *Remain for ever*, Continue throughout eternity. *Under the curse*, To suffer the punishment consequent upon the transgression.

57. *Repentance*, Conviction of, contrition for, and confession of sin. *Amendment of life*, A general improvement of all our moral conduct. *Atone for*, Expiate. *Past sin*, The guilt of those transgressions we had previously committed. *Satisfy*, Appease by paying the full demands of. *Remission*, Forgiveness. *Trusting in*, Depending without doubt upon. *Merits*, Death and intercession. *Helpless*, Weak. *Guilty*, Wicked. *Undone*, Ruined. *Sinners*, Criminals in the sight of God. *Regenerated*, Created anew. *Help*, Assistance. *Thenceforward*, While we continue faithful.

look, even to him that is poor and of a contrite spirit, and trembleth at my word.

5. *We must be regenerated by the Holy Ghost before we can please God and keep his commandments.* John iii. 5. Except a man be born of water, and of the Spirit, he cannot enter into the kingdom of God.

6. *The help of the Holy Ghost is necessary to our pleasing God and keeping his commandments.* Rom. viii. 26. Likewise the Spirit also helpeth our infirmities.

58. *What is a sacrament?*

A sacrament is an *outward and visible sign* of an *inward and spiritual grace given unto us,* which sign is *ordained* by Christ himself, as a *means* whereby *we* receive the grace, and which is a *pledge* to assure *us thereof.*

1. *An inward and spiritual grace is given to believers.* John vi. 56. He that eateth my flesh, and drinketh my blood, dwelleth in me, and I in him.

2. *A sacrament is the outward and visible sign of the inward and spiritual grace which is given to believers.* Luke xxii. 19. And he took bread, and gave thanks, and brake it, and give unto them, saying, This is my body, which is given for you : this do in remembrance of me.

3. *Christ has ordained sacraments as a means of receiving inward and spiritual grace.* 1 Cor. x. 16. The cup of blessing which we bless, is it not the communion of the blood of Christ? the bread which we break, is it not the communion of the body of Christ?

4. *Sacraments are to believers a pledge to assure them of the reception of the grace.* John vi. 51. If any man eat of this bread, he shall live for ever.

59. *How many sacraments hath Christ ordained in his church?*

Christ hath *ordained* two *sacraments in his church,* Baptism and the Lord's Supper.

1. *Christ has ordained in his church the sacrament of baptism.* Matt. xxviii. 19. Go ye therefore, and teach all nations, baptizing them in the name of the Father, and of the Son, and of the Holy Ghost.

2. *Christ has ordained in his church the sacrament of the Lord's supper.* Luke xxii. 19. This do in remembrance of me.

60. *What is Baptism?*

Baptism is the *application of water* in the name of the Father, and of the Son, and of the Holy Ghost, which *sig-*

---

58. *Outward and visible sign,* External symbol, or typical representation, which may be perceived by the bodily senses. *Inward and spiritual grace given unto us,* Internal blessing communicated to the souls of believers, by which they are strengthened and comforted. *Ordained,* Appointed for their observance. *Means,* Medium. *We,* Believers. *Pledge,* Warrant or security. *Assure us,* Satisfy the minds of believers. *Thereof,* That they shall with the sign receive the grace.

59. *Ordained,* Appointed. *Sacraments,* Ordinances in which those who partake of them bind themselves by an oath to be the Lord's. *In his church,* To be observed by his followers.

60. *Application of water,* Being sprinkled with, or immersed in water. *Signifies*

nifies our being *cleansed* from *sin*, and our *becoming new creatures in Christ Jesus;* by which baptism we are *made members* of the *visible church of Christ;* by which baptism our *gracious relation* to *him*, as the *second Adam*, and as the *Mediator* of the *new covenant*, is *solemnly*, and *by divine appointment*, *ratified;* and by which baptism we are *recognised* as having a *claim* to all those spiritual blessings of which baptized persons are the *proper subjects*.

1. *Baptism is the application of water in the name of the Father, and of the Son, and of the Holy Ghost.* Acts viii. 38. They went down both into the water, both Philip and the eunuch; and he baptized him.

2. *Water baptism signifies our being cleansed from sin.* Acts xxii. 16. Arise and be baptised, and wash away thy sins, calling on the name of the Lord.

3. *Water baptism signifies our becoming new creatures in Christ Jesus.* Rom. vi. 3. Know ye not, that so many of us as were baptized into Jesus Christ, were baptised into his death.

4. *By water baptism, we are made members of the visible church of Christ.* Acts ii. 41. Then they that gladly received his word were baptised.

5. *By water baptism, our gracious relation to Christ as the second Adam, and the Mediator of the new covenant, is solemnly ratified.* Matt. iii. 5, 6. Then went out to him, Jerusalem, and all Judea, and all the region round about Jordan; and were baptised of him in Jordan, confessing their sins.

6. *By water baptism, our gracious relation to Christ as the second Adam, and the Mediator of the new covenant, is by divine appointment ratified.* Acts ii. 38. Repent and be baptised every one of you in the name of Jesus Christ.

7. *By water baptism, we are recognised as having a claim to all those spiritual privileges of which baptized persons are the proper subjects.* 1 Cor. xii. 13. For by one Spirit are we all baptised into one body, whether we be Jews or Gentiles, whether we be bond or free.

61. *What does our baptism oblige us to do?*

Our baptism *obliges us* to *renounce* the devil and all *his works*, the pomps and *vanities* of this *wicked world*, and all the *sinful lusts* of the flesh, to *believe* all the *articles* of the

---

Represents. *Cleansed*, Purified. *Sin*, Moral defilement. *Becoming*, Being made. *New creatures in Christ Jesus*, Branches in Christ, the true vine. *Made members*, Admitted to the privileges. *Visible*, Militant. *Church of Christ*, Collective body of Christians. *Gracious relation*, Union through the grace of God. *Him*, Christ. *Second Adam*, Head and representative of believers, as Adam was the representative of all the human race. *Mediator*, Advocate and intercessor. *New covenant*, Gospel dispensation. *Solemnly*, With religious seriousness. *By divine appointment*, In the way commanded by God. *Ratified*, Settled and confirmed. *Recognised*, Acknowledged. *Claim*, Right or title. *Proper*, Fit. *Subjects*, Recipients.

61. *Oblige us*, Makes it our imperative duty. *Renounce*, Quit upon oath. *His works*, Those things which tend to promote his influence. *Pomps*, Unnecessary displays of grandeur. *Vanities*, Follies. *Wicked world*, Present state of existence. *Sinful lusts*, Unholy desires. *Believe*, Give a hearty assent to. *Articles*, Doctrines.

Christian faith, to *keep* God's *holy will* and *commandments,* and to *walk in the same all the days of our lives.*

1. *Our baptism obliges us to renounce the devil.* James iv. 7. Resist the devil, and he will flee from you.

2. *Our baptism obliges us to renounce all the works of the devil.* Eph. v. 11. And have no fellowship with the unfruitful works of darkness, but rather reprove them.

3. *Our baptism obliges us to renounce the pomps of this wicked world.* 1 Tim. ii. 9. In like manner also that women adorn themselves in modest apparel, with shamefacedness and sobriety.

4. *Our baptism obliges us to renounce the vanities of this wicked world.* Col. iii. 2. Set your affections on things above, not on things on the earth.

5. *Our baptism obliges us to renounce all the sinful lusts of the flesh.* 1 Pet. ii. 11. Abstain from fleshly lusts, which war against the soul.

6. *Our baptism obliges us to believe all the articles of the Christian faith.* 1 Tim. ii. 8. I will therefore that men pray everywhere, lifting up holy hands, without wrath and doubting.

7. *Our baptism obliges us to keep God's holy will and commandments.* 2 Tim. ii. 19. Let every one that nameth the name of Christ depart from iniquity.

8. *Our baptism obliges us to walk in God's holy will and commandments all the days of our lives.* Matt. x. 22. He that endureth to the end shall be saved.

62. *What is the Lord's Supper?*

The *outward* part or sign of the Lord's Supper, *is receiving bread and wine,* as Christ has *commanded,* which *signify* the body and blood of Christ, which are spiritually received by *the faithful* in this *ordinance,* to the *strengthening and refreshing of their souls.*

1. *Receiving bread and wine is only the outward part of the Lord's supper.* 1 Cor. xi. 23. The Lord Jesus, the same night in which he was betrayed, took bread, &c.

2. *Christ has commanded bread and wine to be received in the ordinance of the Lord's supper.* Luke xxii. 19. And he took bread, and gave thanks, and brake it, and gave unto them, saying, This is my body which is given for you : this do in remembrance of me. Likewise also the cup after supper, saying, This cup is the new testament in my blood, which is shed for you.

3. *The bread and wine used in the sacrament, signify the body and blood of Christ.* 1 Cor. xi. 26. As often as ye eat this bread, and drink this cup, ye do shew the Lord's death till he come.

4. *The body and blood of Christ are spiritually received by the faithful in the Lord's supper.* 1 Cor. x 16. The cup of blessing which we bless, is it not the communion of the blood of Christ? the bread which break; is it not the communion of the body of Christ?

Christian faith, Old and New Testaments. *Keep,* Obey. *Holy will,* Pure precepts. *Commandments,* Injunctions. *Walk in the same,* Keep them in continued exercise. *All the days of our lives,* During the whole period of our continuance in this world. 62. *Outward,* External. *Receiving bread and wine,* Eating bread and drinking wine. *Commanded,* Ordained and appointed. *Signify,* Represent. *The faithful,* Believers. *Ordinance,* Commanded observance. *Strengthening and refreshing of their souls,* Improvement of their graces, and the comfort of their minds.

5. *The souls of believers are strengthened and refreshed by spiritually receiving the body and blood of Christ in the Lord's supper.* John vi. 55. My flesh is meat indeed, and my blood is drink indeed.

63. *Why ought we to partake of the Lord's Supper?*

We ought to partake of the Lord's Supper *regularly* and *frequently*, in *obedience to* Christ's commandment ; to make a *holy profession* of *Christ and his cross*, by *declaring* our *entire dependence on* his death as the *only atonement* for our *sins*, and as our only *hope of salvation ;* to declare our *love* and *thankfulness* to him, and to enjoy *communion* with God, and with our *fellow-Christians*, in *remembrance* of Christ's death.

1. *We ought to partake of the Lord's supper regularly.* Acts xx. 7. Upon the first day of the week, when the disciples came together to break bread, Paul preached unto them.

2. *We ought to partake of the Lord's supper frequently.* 1 Cor. xi. 26. As often as ye eat this bread, and drink this cup, ye do shew the Lord's death till he come.

3. *We ought to partake of the Lord's supper, in obedience to Christ's commandment.* Luke xxii. 19. This do in remembrance of me.

4. *We ought to partake of the Lord's supper, to make a holy profession of Christ and his cross.* Matt. x. 32. Whosoever therefore shall confess me before men, him will I confess also before my Father which is in heaven.

5. *We ought to make a holy profession of Christ and his cross, by declaring our entire dependence on his death, as the only atonement for our sins.* Acts iv. 12. There is none other name under heaven given among men whereby we must be saved.

6. *We ought to make a holy profession of Christ and his cross, by declaring our entire dependence on his death, as our only hope of salvation.* Acts. iv. 11. This is the stone which was set at nought of you builders, which is become the head of the corner. Neither is there salvation in any other.

7. *We ought to partake of the Lord's supper, to declare our love to Christ.* 1 Cor. xvi. 22. If any man love not the Lord Jesus Christ, let him be Anathema, Maran-atha.

8. *We ought to partake of the Lord's supper, to declare our thankfulness to Christ.* Rev. v. 12. Worthy is the Lamb that was slain to receive power, and riches, and wisdom, and strength, and honour, and glory, and blessing.

9. *We ought to partake of the Lord's supper, to enjoy communion with God.* Matt. xviii. 20. Where two or three are gathered together in my name, there am I in the midst of them.

63. *Regularly*, At stated periods. *Frequently*, With short intervals. *Obedience to*, Compliance with. *Holy*, Sincere and pious, not a thoughtless or hypocritical. *Profession*, Declaration. *Christ and his cross*, Our attachment to Christ, and our belief in the doctrine of his perfect atonement. *Declaring*, Publicly making known. *Entire*, Sole and complete. *Dependence on*, Trust and confidence in. *Only*, Exclusive and certain. *Atonement*, Means of satisfying divine justice. *Sins*, Infractions of the divine law. *Hope*, Ground of expectation. *Salvation*, Deliverance from the power, pollution, and punishment of sin. *Love*, Affection for. *Thankfulness*, Gratitude. *Communion*, Intercourse. *Fellow-Christians*, Christian brethren. *Remembrance*, Commemoration.

10. *We ought to partake of the Lord's supper, to enjoy communion with our fellow Christians in remembrance of Christ's death.* 1 John i. 3. That which we have seen and heard declare we unto you, that ye also may have fellowship with us: and truly our fellowship is with the father, and with his Son Jesus Christ.

64. *What is required of those who come to the Lord's Supper ?*

It is *required of* those who *come to* the Lord's Supper to *examine themselves* whether they *truly repent* of *their former sins,* steadfastly *purposing to lead a new life,* and whether they have *a lively faith* in God's *mercy,* through Christ, with a *thankful remembrance* of his *death,* and are *in charity with* all men.

1. *Those who come to the Lord's supper, must examine themselves whether they truly repent of their former sins.* 1 Cor. xi. 28. Let a man examine himself, and so let him eat of that bread, and drink of that cup.

2. *Those who come to the Lord's supper, must examine themselves whether they steadfastly purpose to lead a new life.* Lam. iii. 40. Let us search and try our ways, and turn again to the Lord.

3. *Those who come to the Lord's supper, must examine themselves whether they have a lively faith in God's mercy through Christ.* 2 Cor. xiii. 5. Examine yourselves whether ye be in the faith.

4. *Those who come to the Lord's supper, must examine themselves whether they have a thankful remembrance of the death of Christ.* 1 Cor. xi. 29. He that eateth and drinketh unworthily, eateth and drinketh damnation to himself, not discerning the Lord's body.

5. *Those who come to the Lord's supper, must examine themselves whether they are in charity with all men.* 1 Cor. v. 8. Therefore let us keep the feast, not with old leaven, neither with the leaven of malice and wickedness, but with the unleavened bread of sincerity and truth.

65. *How are we to use the word of God for our benefit ?*

The word of God, which is contained in the *Scriptures* of the Old and New Testaments, must be *frequently* and *seriously* read and heard, with *prayer* to God, with a *meek* and *teachable disposition,* with *faith,* and with an *intention,* by *God's grace,* to *practise it.*

---

64. *Required of,* Enjoined upon. *Come to,* Present themselves as communicants at. *Examine themselves,* Make serious self inquiry. *Truly,* Unfeignedly, and without reservation. *Repent,* Grieve on account. *Their former sins,* The opposition which they at any time may have felt or manifested to God's law. *Steadfastly,* Firmly. *Purposing,* Resolving by God's grace. *Lead a new life,* Conduct themselves in future in conformity to the divine will. *A lively,* An enlightened and vigorous. *Faith,* Trust and expectation. *Mercy,* Disposition to pardon being exercised in their behalf. *Thankful,* Grateful. *Remembrance,* Recollection. *Death,* Sufferings and crucifixion on their account. *In charity with,* Free from malevolent desires, and willing to promote the happiness of.

65. *Scriptures,* Writings. *Frequently,* Often. *Seriously,* With attentive gravity. *Prayer,* Earnest supplication. *Meek,* Gentle. *Teachable,* Docile. *Disposition,* Inclination of mind. *Faith,* A firm belief of its truth. *Intention,* Fixed determination. *God's grace,* The help of the Holy Spirit. *Practise it,* Perform whatever is commanded therein.

D

1. *The word of God is contained in the Scriptures of the Old and New Testaments.* 1 Thess. ii. 13. When ye received the word of God which ye heard of us, ye received it not as the word of men, but (as it is in truth) the word of God.

2. *The word of God must be read and heard.* John v. 39. Search the Scriptures.

3. *The word of God must be frequently read and heard.* Psalm xix. 7. The law of the Lord is perfect, converting the soul; the testimony of the Lord is sure, making wise the simple.

4. *The word of God must be read and heard with seriousness.* Psalm cxix. 15. I will meditate in thy precepts, and have respect unto thy ways.

5. *The word of God must be read and heard with prayer to God.* Psalm cxix. 18. Open thou mine eyes, that I may behold wondrous things out of thy law.

6. *The word of God must be read and heard with a meek and teachable disposition.* James i. 21. Receive with meekness the ingrafted word, which is able to save your souls.

7. *The word of God must be read and heard with faith.* Heb. iv. 2. The word preached did not profit them, not being mixed with faith in them that heard it.

8. *The word of God must be read and heard with an intention to practise it.* Psalm cxix. 11. Thy word have I hid in mine heart, that I might not sin against thee.

9. *The intention to practise the word of God, should be formed in dependance on God's grace.* 2 Cor. iii. 5. Not that we are sufficient of ourselves to think any thing as of ourselves, but our sufficiency is of God.

66. *What is prayer ?*

Prayer is *an offering up* of our *desires* to God for things *agreeable to his will, in the name* of Christ, with *confession* of our sins, and *thankful acknowledgment of his mercies;* which we are *required* to do in *public, private,* and *secret.*

1. *Prayer is an offering up of our desires to God.* Psalm lxii. 8. Pour out your heart before him; God is a refuge for us.

2. *Prayer is limited to things agreeable to the will of God.* Rom. viii. 27. He maketh intercession for the saints, according to the will of God.

3. *Prayer must be offered to God in the name of Christ.* John xvi.23. Whatsoever ye shall ask the Father in my name, he will give it you.

4. *Prayer must be offered to God with confession of our sins.* Dan. ix. 4. And I prayed unto the Lord my God, and made my confession.

5. *Prayer must be offered to God with thankful acknowledgment of his mercies.* Phil. iv. 6. In every thing by prayer and supplication, with thanksgiving, let your requests be made known unto God.

6. *We are required to pray to God in public.* Psalm c. 4. Enter into his gates with thanksgiving, and into his courts with praise.

66. *An offering up,* A presenting or spreading out *Desires,* Earnest wishes. *Agreeable to his will,* In accordance with what he has promised in his word. *In the name,* For the sake. *Confession,* Penitential acknowledgment. *Thankful acknowledgment of his mercies,* Feelings and expressions of gratitude for all the spiritual and temporal favours which he has bestowed upon us. *Required,* Commanded. *Public,* The assemblies of God's people in the church. *Private,* The family, or privately amongst friends. *Secret,* Alone, or in the closet.

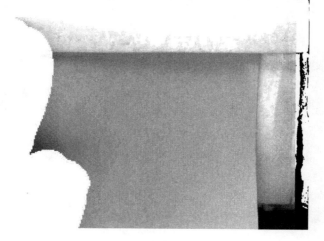

7. *We are required to pray to God in private.* Jer. x. 25. Pour out thy fury upon the heathen that know thee not, and upon the families that call not on thy name.

8. *We are required to pray to God in secret.* Matt. vi. 6. But thou, when thou prayest, enter into thy closet; and, when thou hast shut thy door, pray to thy Father which is in secret; and thy Father, which seeth in secret, shall reward thee openly.

67. *What rule hath God given for our direction in prayer?*

The whole *word of God* is *of use* to *direct* us in prayer, but the *special rule of direction* is that *form* of prayer which Christ taught his *disciples, commonly called* the Lord's prayer

1. *The whole word of God is of use to direct us in prayer.* 1 John v. 14. And this is the confidence that we have in him, that if we ask any thing according to his will, he heareth us.

2. *The Lord's prayer is the special rule given for our direction in prayer.* Luke xi. 2. When ye pray, say, Our Father which art in heaven, &c.

68. *Repeat the Lord's Prayer.*

Our Father which art in heaven, Hallowed be thy name, Thy kingdom come, Thy will be done in earth as it is in heaven. Give us this day our daily bread, and forgive us our trespasses, as we forgive them that trespass against us, and lead us not into temptation, but deliver us from evil; for thine is the kingdom, and the power, and the glory, for ever and ever. Amen.

69. *What doth the preface of our Lord's prayer teach us?*

The *preface of* our Lord's prayer, which is, " Our Father which art in heaven," teaches us to *draw near to God* with all *holy reverence* and *confidence*, as children to a father, able and ready to help us, and that we should pray *with*, and *for* others.

1. *We are in prayer to approach God with holy reverence.* Isa. lxiv. 9. Be not wroth very sore, O Lord, neither remember iniquity for ever: behold, see, we beseech thee, we are all thy people.

2. *We are in prayer to approach God with holy confidence.* 1 John v. 14. And this is the confidence that we have in him, that if we ask any thing according to his will, he heareth us.

3. *We are in prayer to approach God as our Father.* Rom. viii. 15. Ye have received the spirit of adoption, whereby we cry, Abba, Father.

---

67. *Word of God,* Bible. *Of use,* Useful. *Direct,* Guide or instruct. *Special, Particular. Rule of direction,* Standard for our help and imitation. *Form,* Model or example. *Disciples,* Scholars or followers. *Commonly called,* Generally named.

68. (The Lord's prayer.)

69. *Preface of,* Introduction to. *Draw near to God,* Come into the presence of God in the exercise of prayer. *Holy reverence,* Sincere and pious respect and awe. *Confidence,* A firm trust and reliance on his promised mercy. *With,* In company with. *For,* In behalf of.

4. *We are in prayer to approach God as being able to help us.* Eph. iii. 20. Unto him that is able to do exceeding abundantly above all that we ask or think.

5. *We are in prayer to approach God as being ready to help us.* Luke xi. 13. How much more shall your heavenly Father give the Holy Spirit to them that ask him?

6. *We are to join with others in prayer.* Acts xii. 12. Many were gathered together praying.

7. *We are to pray for others.* 1 Tim. ii. 1. I exhort therefore, that first of all, supplications, prayers, intercessions, and giving of thanks, be made for all men.

70. *What do we pray for in the first petition?*

In the first *petition,* which is, " *Hallowed* be thy name," we pray that God would *enable* us and others to *glorify him* in all that, *whereby he maketh himself known,* and that he would *dispose* all things *to his own glory.*

1. *We pray God to enable us to glorify him.* Psalm li. 15. O Lord, open thou my lips; and my mouth shall shew forth thy praise.

2. *We pray God to enable others to glorify him.* Psalm lxvii. 5. Let the people praise thee, O God. Let all the people praise thee.

3. *We pray God to dispose all things to his own glory.* John xii. 28. Father, glorify thy name.

71. *What do we pray for in the second petition?*

In the second petition, which is, " Thy kingdom come," we pray that *Satan's kingdom* may be *destroyed,* that the *kingdom of grace* may be *advanced,* ourselves and others brought into it, and *kept in it,* and that the *kingdom of glory* may be *hastened.*

1. *We pray that Satan's kingdom may be destroyed.* Psalm lxviii. 1. Let God arise, let his enemies be scattered; let them also that hate him flee before him.

2. *We pray that the kingdom of grace may be advanced.* Psalm li. 18. Do good in thy good pleasure unto Zion: build thou the walls of Jerusalem.

3. *We pray that we may be brought into the kingdom of grace.* Psalm lxxi. 2. Incline thine ear unto me, and save me.

4. *We pray that others may be brought into the kingdom of grace.* Rom. x. 1. Brethren, my heart's desire and prayer to God for Israel is, that they might be saved.

5. *We pray that we and others may be kept in the kingdom of grace.*

---

70. *Petition,* Request. *Hallowed,* Sanctified or holy. *Enable,* Effectually help. *Glorify him,* Shew forth his glory. *Whereby,* By which. *Maketh himself known,* Reveals himself and his doings to his rational creatures. *Dispose,* Arrange and regulate. *To his own glory,* To promote his designs, and to make known the glory of his infinite perfections.

71. *Satan's kingdom,* The power and dominion of the devil in this world. *Destroyed,* Put an end to. *Kingdom of grace,* Dominion of Christ in the hearts of men by the gracious influences of the Holy Spirit. *Advanced,* Brought forward, and make greater progress towards perfection. *Kept in it,* Preserved from ever falling away from a state of grace. *Kingdom of glory,* Glorious reign of Christ with his people in heaven after the last day. *Hastened,* Made to come with greater speed, and in a short time.

2 Thess. iii. 1. Brethren, pray for us, that the word of the Lord may have free course, and be glorified, even as it is with you.

6. *We pray that the kingdom of glory may be hastened.* Rev. xxii. 20. He which testifieth these things saith, Surely I come quickly: Amen. Even so come, Lord Jesus.

72. *What do we pray for in the third petition ?*

In the third petition, which is, " Thy will be done in earth as it is in heaven," we pray that God, by his *grace*, would make us able and willing *to know, obey*, and *submit to his will in all things*, as the angels do in heaven.

1. *We pray that God would make us able and willing to know his will.* Psalm cxix. 36. Incline my heart unto thy testimonies.

2. *We pray that God would make us able and willing to obey his will.* Psalm cxix. 35. Make me to go in the path of thy commandments, for therein do I delight.

3. *We pray that God would make us able and willing to submit to his will in all things, as the angels do in heaven.* Job i. 21. The Lord gave, and the Lord hath taken away ; blessed be the name of the Lord.

73. *What do we pray for in the fourth petition ?*

In the fourth petition, which is, " Give us this day our daily bread," we pray that of God's *free gift* we may receive a *competent portion* of the good things of this life, and *enjoy his blessing* with them.

1. *We pray that God would give us a competent portion of the good things of this life.* Prov. xxx. 8. Give me neither poverty nor riches ; feed me with food convenient for me.

2. *We pray that we may enjoy the blessing of God together with the good things of this life.* Prov. x. 22. The blessing of the Lord it maketh rich, and he addeth no sorrow with it.

74. *What do we pray for in the fifth petition ?*

In the fifth petition, which is, " And forgive us our *trespasses*, as we forgive them that *trespass against us*," we pray that God, for Christ's sake, would *freely* pardon all our sins, which we are the rather *encouraged* to ask, because by his grace we are *enabled from the heart* to forgive others.

1. *We pray that God would freely pardon all our sins.* Psalm li. 1. Have mercy upon me, O God, according to thy loving kindness : according unto the multitude of thy tender mercies, blot out my transgressions.

2. *We pray that God for Christ's sake would freely pardon all our.*

72. *Grace*, Favour and help. *To know*, Honestly and diligently to use the means by which we shall become acquainted with his will. *Obey*, Faithfully and constantly to do all that we know to be his will. *Submit to his will in all things*, Cheerfully to yield to, and bear up under all his dispensations.

73. *Free gift*, Goodness in freely giving what we have no right to demand. *Competent portion*, Suitable part. *Enjoy*, Happily possess. *His blessing*, His friendship and love.

74. *Trespasses*, Offences against thee. *Trespass against us*, Injure or offend us. *Freely*, Frankly of his goodness. *Encouraged*, Emboldened and incited. *Enabled*, Successfully helped. *From the heart*, Sincerely, and with all our heart.

sins. Rom. iii. 24. Being justified freely by his grace, through the redemption that is in Christ Jesus.

3. *We are encouraged to ask the forgiveness of our sins, by the feeling that God by his grace has enabled us from the heart to forgive others.* Luke xi. 4. Forgive us our sins, for we also forgive every one that is indebted to us.

75. *What do we pray for in the sixth petition?*

In the sixth petition, which is, " And lead us not into *temptation*, but *deliver us from evil*," we pray that God would either keep us from being brought into such circumstances as will *specially tempt* us to sin, or *support* and *deliver us* when we are tempted.

1. *We pray God to keep us from circumstances which would tempt us to sin.* Matt. xxvi. 41. Watch and pray that ye enter not into temptation.

2. *We pray God to support us when we are tempted.* Psalm li. 12. Uphold me with thy free Spirit.

3. *We pray God to deliver us when we are tempted.* 2 Cor. xii. 8. For this thing I besought the Lord thrice, that it might depart from me.

76. *What does the conclusion of the Lord's Prayer teach us?*

The *conclusion* of the Lord's Prayer, wich is, " For thine is the kingdom, and the power, and the glory, for ever, Amen," teacheth us to take our *encouragement* in prayer from God only, and in our prayers to praise him, *ascribing* kingdom, power, and glory to him; and *in testimony* of our *desire* and *assurance to be heard*, we say, *Amen.*

1. *We are to take our encouragement in prayer from God only.* Dan. ix. 18. We do not present our supplications before thee for our righteousness, but for thy great mercies.

2. *We are to praise God in our prayers.* 1. Chron. xxix. 13. Now therefore, our God, we thank thee, and praise thy glorious name.

3. *We are to ascribe kingdom, power, and glory to God.* 1 Chron. xxix. 11. Thine, O Lord, is the greatness, and the power, and the glory, and the victory, and the majesty; for all that is in the heaven and in the earth is thine.

4. *We say Amen to our prayers in testimony of our desire and assurance to be heard.* Rev. xxii. 20. Amen. Even so come, Lord Jesus.

77. *What are we to understand respecting death?*

Death is the *separation* of the *soul* from the *body*; all men

---

75. *Temptation*, A situation in which we may be inclined or persuaded to sin. *Deliver us from evil*, Save us from being guilty of any improper or sinful act, and also from the snares of the evil one. *Specially*, Particularly. *Tempt*, Induce or dispose. *Support*, Enable us to resist. *Deliver us*, Rescue us from the danger of our situation.

76. *Conclusion*, Last part or ending. *Encouragement*, Incitements and confidence. *Ascribing*, Acknowledging to be his due, and attributing. *In testimony*, As a proof. *Desire*, Sincere wish. *Assurance to be heard*, Certain conviction and belief of being heard. *Amen*, So be it, or let it be.

77. *Separation*, Disunion or removal. *Soul*, Immaterial and immortal spirit.

will die except those who shall be *alive* at Christ s *second coming*. *Christians* only are not afraid to die, because sin, which is *the sting of death*, is *taken away from them*, and they *know* that after death they shall go to *heaven*.

1. *Death is the separation of the soul from the body.* Eccles. xii. 7. Then shall the dust return to the earth as it was, and the spirit shall return unto God who gave it.

2. *Those persons who are alive at Christ's second coming, will not die.* 1 Thess. iv. 17. Then we which are alive and remain, shall be caught up together with them in the clouds to meet the Lord in the air; and so shall we ever be with the Lord.

3. *All men will die except those who shall be alive at Christ's second coming.* Heb. ix. 27. It is appointed unto men once to die.

4. *Christians are the only persons who are not afraid to die.* Phil. i. 23. For I am in a strait betwixt two, having a desire to depart, and to be with Christ, which is far better.

5. *Christians are not afraid to die, because sin, which is the sting of death, has been taken away from them.* 1 Cor. xv. 56, 57. The sting of death is sin, and the strength of sin is the law. But thanks be to God, which giveth us the victory through our Lord Jesus Christ.

6. *Christians are not afraid to die, because they know that after death they shall go to heaven.* 2 Cor. v. 1. For we know, that if our earthly house of this tabernacle were dissolved, we have a building of God, an house not made with hands, eternal in the heavens.

78. *What shall happen at the end of the world?*

When all the *prophecies* in *God's holy word* shall have *been accomplished*, and when the *gospel* shall have been *preached* to all *nations*, Jesus Christ will *suddenly come* in *pomp* and great *glory* to *judge* all *mankind*. The *dead* shall be *raised*, and with those who *are then alive*, shall stand before him. He will *reveal* and judge all the *actions* of men. He will place *the righteous* on his right hand, and the *wicked* on his left, *sentence* shall then be *openly pronounced*. The

Body, Outward frame of flesh and bones inhabited by it while in this world. *Alive,* In existence upon the earth. *Second coming,* Appearance at the day of judgment. *Christians,* Those who believe in Christ, and are his followers. *The sting of death,* That which renders death most to be dreaded. *Taken away from them,* Pardoned and washed away in the blood of Christ. *Know,* Are assured by the Spirit of God which dwelleth in them. *Heaven,* The place of God's more immediate presence, where peace and joy are ever found.

78. *Prophecies,* Predictions, or things foretold. *God's holy word,* The Bible. *Been accomplished,* Come to pass. *Gospel,* Glad tidings of salvation by a Redeemer *Preached,* Proclaimed and made known. *Nations,* People. *Suddenly,* Unexpectedly, and in a moment. *Come,* Descend from heaven. *Pomp,* Splendour. *Glory,* Honour and dignity. *Judge,* Try the merits of. *Mankind,* The inhabitants of this world who have lived in every generation. *Dead,* Dust of the dead bodies of all mankind, who shall have ever lived upon the earth. *Raised,* Made to rise up after their particles have been collected and put into their respective forms. *Are then alive,* Shall happen to be alive upon the earth at that time. *Reveal,* Make known to the whole world. *Actions,* Deeds. *The righteous,* Those who shall have accepted his offers of mercy, and complied with the terms of salvation. *Wicked,* Ungodly sinners and wicked spirits. *Sentence,* The solemn final decision of reward and punishment. *Openly pronounced,* Declared in the hearing and presence of the

world shall be *destroyed by fire.* The wicked shall *go away into everlasting punishment,* but the righteous shall go into *life eternal.*

1. *All the prophecies contained in God's word must be accomplished prior to Christ's coming to judgment.* Matt. v. 18. Till heaven and earth pass, one jot or one tittle shall in no wise pass from the law, till all be fulfilled.

2. *The gospel must be preached among all nations prior to Christ's coming to judgment.* Matt. xxiv. 14. And this gospel of the kingdom shall be preached in all the world, for a witness unto all nations; and then shall the end come.

3. *When all the prophecies shall have been accomplished, and when the gospel shall have been preached to all nations, Jesus Christ will come to judge all mankind.* Acts. xvii. 31. He hath appointed a day in the which he will judge the world in righteousness, by that man whom he hath ordained.

4. *Jesus Christ will come suddenly to judge all mankind.* 1 Thess. v. 2. The day of the Lord so cometh as a thief in the night.

5. *Jesus Christ will come in pomp and great glory to judge all mankind.* Matt xvi. 27. The Son of man shall come in the glory of his Father, with his angels; and then he shall reward every man according to his works.

6. *The dead shall be raised at the day of judgment.* Acts xxiv. 15. There shall be a resurrection of the dead, both of the just and unjust.

7. *The raised dead shall stand before Christ at the judgment.* Rev. xx. 12. I saw the dead, small and great, stand before God.

8. *The persons who are alive at the coming of Christ, shall stand before him at the judgment.* Rev. i. 7. Behold he cometh with clouds; and every eye shall see him, and they also which pierced him.

9. *Christ will reveal and judge all the actions of men.* Eccles. xii. 14. God shall bring every work into judgment, with every secret thing, whether it be good or whether it be evil.

10 *Christ will place the righteous on his right hand, and the wicked on his left hand in the judgment.* Matt. xxv. 32, 33. He shall separate them, one from another, as a shepherd divideth his sheep from the goats; and he shall set the sheep on his right hand, but the goats on the left.

11. *At the judgment, sentence shall be openly pronounced.* Matt. xxv. 41. Then shall he say also unto them on the left hand, Depart, ye cursed, into everlasting fire.

12. *After the judgment, the world shall be destroyed by fire.* 2 Pet. iii. 10. The heavens shall pass away with a great noise, and the elements shall melt with fervent heat; the earth also, and the works that are therein, shall be burnt up.

13. *After the judgment, the wicked shall go away into everlasting punishment.* Psalm ix. 17. The wicked shall be turned into hell, and all the nations that forget God.

14. *After the judgment, the righteous shall go away into life eternal.* Matt. xxv. 46. These shall go away into everlasting punishment, but the righteous into life eternal.

whole assembled multitude. *Destroyed by fire,* Consumed or melted down by intense heat. *Go away,* Be cast down. *Everlasting punishment,* Endless misery and torment. *Life eternal,* Happiness interminable.

THE END.

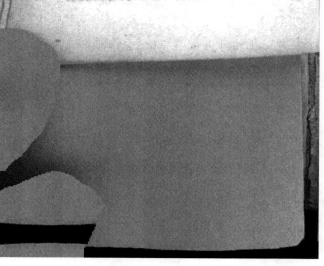

Printed in the USA
CPSIA information can be obtained
at www.ICGtesting.com
LVHW021454241223
767345LV00004B/106